The Hypocrisy Of

America

Table of Contents

Dedications

This book is dedicated to all my friends, and family. I appreciate you all.

For all those who died or have lost a loved one to cancer or any other horrible disease.

For all those who are fighting for justice.

For all those fighting for freedom.

For all those who feel powerless.

For those who are helping others.

For all of us who suffered during the Covid pandemic from issues real and imagined.

For all of us who were ostracized for no logical reason for not being vaccinated.

I have a t-shirt company called Tortured Tees. The motto is, "Tortured Tees, for the tortured soul in all of us." I feel we all have our own inner demons we battle. Even when we look like we have everything together, and we are happy, some of us have a daily battle we fight with ourselves. This book is for you too.

www.facebook.com/torturedtees

AMERICA: THE WAR MACHINE

Forward by Kenneth Cosentino

James and I have been friends for a long time now; I met him right after he got out of federal prison. We met at his brother's boxing gym located above a tattoo parlor. He was quiet, reserved, a hell of a fighter, and observant of everything that was going on in the room. Today we own a company together, White Lion Studios, LLC, and we both founded the original company Little Sicily Productions in 2009. Last year, I ran a political campaign in my hometown for the only grassroots candidate on the slate; Bill Kennedy, our company president and brother. Bill won top vote and is now a seated Niagara Falls city councilman. Together we unseated Governor Andrew Cuomo's publicly endorsed eight-year incumbent. What is a state governor doing interfering with local city elections and how many cities in New York State, come election time, can say that Cuomo sends money, people and resources to support a candidate? Truth be told the whole system is corrupt and I saw it first hand in my dealings with politicians and their handlers on many levels. Running a political campaign became more of a revolution as we played a big game of chess with the professionals who put politicians in office for a living. With Bill as our candidate, we won that chess game. James taught me how to play chess. He also introduced me to the musical stylings of Tom Waits, so right there you are either going to love this book or hate it.

While reading the book, I picture James telling me this story from the boxing gym, or inside a prison cell, or in a courtroom. His writing style flows from a passionate and well-informed rant; to a personal journey full of lessons; to board room brawler - Wolf of Wall Street motherfucker - with a narrative reminiscent of Goodfellas. Let me tell you - this guy is dangerous. He's dangerous in a sense that he knows what the fuck he's talking about and he's not going to limit his words, or play to the egos of public figures. I have spent time in a boxing ring with James and we've gone to war together on several of our film productions. Few people are as knowledgeable as he is about what's going on in our country and society. He's got his finger on the pulse of corruption and with this book it looks like he's going to strangle it.

The first thing I can think of to tell you is: Follow the money trail. Corporations are running this country. Hell, the United States of America is a corporation located around Washington D.C. In 1791, the District of Columbia was ceded to the federal government for the purpose of becoming the nation's capital, to be governed by Congress. What's the opposite of Progress? Congress. According to the 10th Amendment of the Constitution, all powers not granted to the federal government are reserved for the states and the people. D.C. residents have only been able to vote for President since 1964. Whereas states appoint their own judges, the President appoints judges for District Court.

The President acts as CEO of the American Corporation, but the biggest problem is the Federal Reserve. We are borrowing money from private bankers who trade us bonds with interest. If we borrow $100 and they print all of our money, they have to print an additional debt to pay the interest. So our country is perpetually in debt, it's not broken; it's how the system was designed. It is a system of debt and after FDR's New Deal, we became collateral. The reason we have social security and a national census is so the government knows how much the country is worth in assets because we are weighed against the World Stock Exchange. We the taxpayers support this ridiculous shit and the result is the decimation of the class system from upper, middle and lower to upper, working class and poor. These are the final days of capitalism and 1% of the most elite billionaires in the world are collecting all debts.

I say this with utmost assurance given the gravity of the situation; Donald Trump is President of the United States of America. Capitalism as we know it will not survive climate change. Much of our economy is supported by energy companies in the coal and oil businesses, and these same moguls are the ones pulling the strings globally. Lobbyists and unions are both corrupted and both have more political sway than every man, woman and child on this soil. The system is not broken, it is designed to be a Democratic front for capitalism. Capitalism has poisoned our Democracy. Money is not the root of all evil; the love of money is. These same corporations are mega-conglomerates and they also own most major media outlets, Hollywood, and they're partnered with banks. I worked as a legal assistant at a law firm that handles mortgages, bankruptcies and foreclosures. At that time, I saw the bowels of the ship we call America. I saw how banks open lending services with appealing titles like Financial Freedom and The Money Source. My job was to proofread documents and I was absolutely floored when I read the authentication stamps from certain banks which stated "BIG BANK UNDER THE FICTITIOUS NAME OF AMERICAN WHOLESALE LENDER." How does one sell mortgages wholesale?

Lawyers and office managers spoke openly about the absolute corruption, but most showed no remorse for the borrowers because "They shouldn't have signed the contract." I saw the inner workings of the systems compiling all of the data for every single borrower from every bank that the firm worked with. Basically it was a collection agency and the lowest rung of work for an attorney. Banks own the property and the borrower takes out a bank loan to purchase the property from the bank. Let's say a house is sold for $100,000; you take out a mortgage to pay for the $100,000 but the full loan is not given to you - the house is. So you don't really see a penny of that loan but you pay it with interest in order to live in the house. Banks don't have money to loan out, they use our money. These days it's all digital so who knows if that money is actually sitting in the bank or if there is a CEO somewhere on their yacht surrounded by high priced hookers. Half of my time at the law firm was spent in the vault and I imagined myself setting fire to everyone's mortgages. I probably would have done it too, had I not been told that the original document was no longer necessary for the mortgage to remain valid (they have something called a "lost note affidavit" which ruined my diabolical scheme).

The banks may own the property, but the government claims ownership over the land. Land ownership is the biggest scam and the most common form of colonization right after raping and pillaging. Soon comes enslavement; whether it be slaves in shackles or wage slaves, the difference is the former know they are shackled. Along with enslavement comes conformity (the United States educational institution is just as corrupt as the healthcare system) preying off of the sick is, in itself, a mental illness. So who is it that is perpetrating this mental illness? Psychopaths. The world is run by psychopaths who lack empathy; and so, when made aware that their new pipeline will run through protected land and poison the only water source for the Natives, the CEO for Big Oil doesn't flinch. Truthfully, it's all about Manifest Destiny. It's still going on today, right in front of our eyes. Race wars, the war on drugs, terrorism; all of it is meant to fuel America's number 1 export: War. If I had written this book, I would have called it "America: The War Machine" because that's what it all boils down to. Our main business is conquering other countries, assassinating their leaders and installing Democratic Capitalism. The long arm of Johnny Law extends overseas in our military industrial complex. We produce bullets, missiles, planes, tanks, bombs, etc. and then we create the need for more! Supply and demand, business is booming.

So then, what can we do about all of this? Well first and foremost we must be informed of our rights and well informed of what the hell is going on. The government does not give us our rights, we are born with rights. The government is "supposed" to protect those rights. It says so right in the Constitution. That's what the whole Democracy "thing" is "supposed" to be about. Historically, different dynasties have held power within this system. The Bushes, Clintons, Rothschilds, etc. are all dynasties. The Clinton Dynasty took a devastating blow from Donald Trump who is representing his rich friends that are sucking what little life is left from our economy.

This book does an excellent job of bringing the uninformed, average individual up to date with the reality that we are currently experiencing. Consider this: If you were in charge, would you still be following the 40 hour work week? Why would we create a system, based on 24 hours a day, where we are meant to sleep 8 hours, work 8 hours and have 8 hours of recreation? Does it actually work this way? Hell no, it does not! People typically get less than 8 hours of sleep, work more than 8 hours a day and spend the rest of their time drunk, on drugs or zoned out in front of the television, trying to ignore the piling debt from being taxed to death. This is how they keep you sedated so that you don't revolt. Who has time to start a revolution when we all have nine-to-fives and bills to pay? Why is it illegal to collect rainwater? What the fuck is that about?! It falls from the sky and it collects naturally, but if we put out a barrel to catch it and store it, somebody's gotta get paid??

The 13th Amendment states: Neither slavery nor involuntary servitude, except as a punishment for crime whereof the party shall have been duly convicted, shall exist within the United States or any place subject to their jurisdiction. Slavery still exists today, it's just made legal by unjust conviction. James does an excellent job of explaining this fact from the point of view of someone who was "inside."

December 4th, 2016, former President Obama halted the Dakota Access Pipeline (DAPL) after public outcry in support of the Standing Rock Water Protectors safety. Of course, it was just a show of humanity on his part. It didn't stick. January 24th, 2017, President Trump reversed the halt, expediting the environmental review which he described as an "incredibly cumbersome, long, horrible permitting process." On February 7th, Trump authorized the Army Corps of Engineers to proceed. February 23rd, law enforcement assisted by the National Guard evicted anyone who was left at Standing Rock. DAPL was constructed, declaring victories for the untouchable elite billionaires who invested in Energy Transfer Partners and the pipeline (including Trump himself); vicious mercenaries such as TigerSwan who declared war on Sioux soil against American citizens gathering in protest and prayer; and the outright racist Morton County justice (Just Us) department who saw an opportunity to beat up some Indians. In all of that, when these events were happening in real time, on January 21st and 22nd an estimated 500,000–1,000,000 people protested in Washington, D.C. at the Women's Rights March. It was an anti-Trump extravaganza where women dressed in gigantic pink foam vagina costumes and shouted their disapproval that *he is not their president*. Had these people instead rerouted to Standing Rock where those at the front needed them, history would be different. Hillary fans were in it for the photo opportunity, but there are those of us who actually want to see change in the status quo.

So, I will leave you with this: Vote with your dollar. If you are endorsing corporations that are destroying our planet and making us sick, find a small privately owned company to buy from instead. Keep money circulating locally by shopping with local businesses. Take this book, not as entertainment, but as a guide to bettering your life. Remove the rose-colored glasses from your face and join the revolution, we need all the help that we can get. What Mr. Ventry has done here by compiling data and citing all of his sources is a great service to the betterment of mankind, and I'm proud to call him my brother.

~ *Ken Cosentino* 11/27/2018

!

Introduction

I started thinking about writing this book during the first Bush administration. As what often happens with me, I get inspired or angry, and then the feeling goes away or other projects get in the way, and I never end up following through. As each issue sort of came and went, I would always think, "well, you blew it, your book idea won't be relevant now." Sadly though, month after month, year after year the premise of this book keeps being relevant. Now here we are some 4+ years later and there is just so much more to write about. The more things change, the more they stay the same. I'm writing the second edition to "The Hypocrisy of America" and I will add content throughout each chapter while adding a chapter on 'covid" and all the nefarious bs that went on during that nightmare. I was going to eliminate the chapter on "Trump, Hillary and Bernie", but I decided to keep the chapter in, add a little and just inform the reader some of the information was much more relevant when Trump was in office and if you are a Bernie fan I think you will enjoy it, although I will be adding some criticism of Mr. Sanders.

The main premise of this book is to dispel a myth we are taught as children. It's an idea that is implanted in us and to a large extent we are brainwashed with this idea. At some point in our lives, many of us come to realize that what we were taught was the ultimate truth was nothing more than the ultimate lie. What is this myth? It's the simple belief that everything America does is just. If we are doing something as a nation, it must be "just" because it's for the betterment of the world. We're America, home of the brave, land of the free. We're America, the freest country in the world. We're America, we set the standard for human rights. We're America, the red, white, and blue my friend. We wouldn't be doing something if it weren't right;

Right? Some people, somehow, never open their eyes to the realization this is only a myth. I'm referring to the Bill O'Reilly's, the Rush Limbaugh's; every right wing, conservative Republican; every blue loving, no-matter-what voting Democrat; every gun-toting hillbilly and, well, actually, almost everyone.

I think very few people have the ability to see the truth. I even see it with the tribalism of being either a Republican or a Democrat, and tribalism attached to one Party or the other has gotten worse than ever. One of my biggest complaints about Trump supporters was facts meant nothing to them, and now with Covid Democrats and many on the left are in the exact same boat and just as the Trump supporters they don't even know it. Most individuals blindly go on believing in the righteousness of America. They believe in our government's right to incarcerate endless amounts of Americans without having to prove their crimes. Well, Rush Limbaugh may have changed his mind about this after his little prescription drug charges, but probably only when it concerns himself. They believe in our right to detain individuals in the name of national security while believing those detained do not even have the right to know why or how long they are being detained for. They believe in our right to invade foreign countries or overthrow governments who won't allow our corporations to steal their natural resources, but not in our right as citizens to question those reasons or the right. They believe in our government's right to strip the constitution of all its meaning while boasting we are the freest country in the world. During the pandemic they believed in the government's right to force people to inject something in their bodies. So much for my body, my choice.

Even U.S. citizens don't seem to be in favor of freedoms when it's someone else who does not share the same belief as them. From liberals who protest speakers they disagree with to the typical slightly racist individuals who were so angry at those kneeling during our national anthem. Oh, and now with having gone through the Covid pandemic I'm absolutely blown away at how easily people gave up their freedoms, especially those on the left. So many individuals were and still are completely brainwashed when it comes to Covid and if they don't hear it from their side, they refuse to believe it. When I first started thinking about writing this book I was planning on starting with our governments policy of genocide towards Native Americans, and working my way up to slavery, and the black mark on our constitution. I would continue my writing with in depth looks at all our immoral acts as a country. That would have been a book written similar to an author like Stephen Ambrose, but obviously much more critical of the U.S. than Mr. Ambrose ever wrote. I love political commentary, and satire. Being big fans of both Michael Moore, and Al Franken I decided to write a book more in their style. I thought it would have broader appeal, allow me to focus on subjects that are more important to me, and lastly give me an opportunity to call people like Rush Limbaugh, Sean Hannity, Tucker Carlson and of course Donald Trump and Hilliary Clinton all assholes. In doing so, not only would I have fun, but possibly Michael and Al would become fans of mine.

I thought living through the Bush years was bad. I even broke up with a girlfriend I was going out with because she thought he was a great President. No matter how hard I tried I couldn't get it through her head that Iraq had nothing to do with the 9/11 attacks. With the creation of the Patriot Act we lost some freedoms under President Bush. Free speech was under attack big time. On April 23rd 2004 Secret Service agents interrogated a 15 year old high school student in Prosser, Washington for making anti-war sketches for his art class. This is the sort of thing you think about happening in communist China, not the United States of America. Thomas Jefferson once said "A society that will trade a little liberty for a little order will deserve neither and lose both." I thought the attack on free speech was bad during the Bush years, but Bush doesn't have shit on Joe Biden and his administration with all the censorship which has taken place during Covid. All information that went against the government's narrative was surpassed. Think about that statement. It's not my opinion and it also not just done on mainstream media. If you had a YouTube channel and you said anything that went against the government narrative you were shut right down. Controlling information is key to controlling the population. The government needs an uninformed, uneducated society in order to do as it pleases. In general President Trump made me long for President Bush, and President Biden makes me long to be someone who just doesn't care (although Bush/Cheney did far more real world damage than President Trump ever did), and free speech is something President Trump is only in favor of if he likes who is speaking, and what they are saying. The act of kneeling would be considered free speech, and we know how Trump felt about that. I would never burn the flag, but I don't think it should be against the law either. Trump once tweeted "Nobody should be allowed to burn the American flag – if they do, there must be consequences – perhaps loss of citizenship or a year in jail!" Worse than all of that, President Trump has called journalists an "enemy of the American People." Wow, no President should ever feel comfortable with saying such nonsense. Although, there never has been another President more comfortable with uttering more nonsense than President Trump.

I'm not writing this book for scholars who already know much of this information. I'm writing it for the slightly above average, curious, American. I wrote "slightly above average" American because I'm afraid so many Americans have given up and are completely disengaged from the political process. In all honesty I am so close to quitting myself so I definitely understand how many people feel. I love my country. That being said, I don't love it blindly, and I certainly have zero trust for our government. Most people have zero trust in our government, but for some reason when it came to Covid they believed our government and the pharmaceutical companies without question. This is not the country our four fathers envisioned. We have lost freedoms, and are becoming more and more of a totalitarian state every day. In Trump we had a fascist leader with a cult-like following who were clearly unable to think for themselves at all. Currently Joe Biden is the President and maybe he doesn't put out offensive tweets, but in general his Presidency has been a huge disappointment. We are in more danger than ever of moving further, and further away from our American myth.

You may not agree with this because you get to watch your television, drink your beer, and for the most part no one bothers you, although during the lockdowns you couldn't do shit, but most Americans didn't seem to mind those loss of freedoms. Now we really have to be careful with the government using news organizations and controlling social media to silence anyone who disagrees with them, often labeling the difference of opinion as "misinformation". When the government is deciding what is misinformation and what isn't then the truth is lost forever. I have a house in Niagara Falls that I had on Airbnb for a short period of time, and I met people from countries such as Italy, India, Canada, Spain, and France to name a few, and they all told me this is the most policed nation they have ever visited. From the time you wake up to the time you go to bed, to the time you wake up again there is no aspect of your life the government does not touch. You may not be aware, and of course much of what they regulate is good, but there is no doubt the government is ever present in our lives. Besides working for corporations, our government runs, and supports the two most immoral jobs programs there are in the Military Industrial Complex, and the Prison Industrial Complex. We have approximately 25% of the world's prison population while only representing just under 5% of the world's population. As Americans, we are either the worst lot of people on the face of the planet or our government is way too intrusive. It's one or the other, so which is it?

The ideals of this country are beautiful. With every civil liberty lost this country loses some of its beauty. With every individual locked up for long periods of time for minor crimes this country loses some of its humanity. With every act of tyranny throughout the world our government loses some of its credibility. As a society if we don't step up, and make our government accountable, then the dream of America will be just that, a dream, and the myth of America will forever be our reality.

Chapter 1-

Covid Conspiray's

I moved to Los Angeles, CA in December of 2019. It was fantastic not having to be in Western NY for the winter and I was excited for new opportunities. I met my best friend Wadi Abdellatif, his girlfriend and my good friend Jamie DePetris, as well as Wadi's cousin Yazan Talab. We had a great week or so then they went back home to Niagara Falls, NY while I remained behind. I'm a part owner of a film production company called White Lion Studios and being in a small film production company we all have to wear many hats. One of the hats I've been lucky enough to wear is that of an actor. My biggest role was that of Tommy Emerson in Crimson the Motion Picture. I played the lead antagonist and although it was my first time acting with a lot of help from director Ken Cosentino I have to say I did a pretty good job. The film did fairly well and even landed on the shelves of Best Buy. I didn't come to Los Angeles to be an actor, but I figured while I was here I would try to get some auditions and see what happened. As I started searching for possible roles and got everything together I landed my first two auditions both set for early April. Then as March rolled in something weird happened. Cases of Covid which I had heard a little about started to rise and quickly governments took unprecedented action and started shutting businesses down. Both my auditions were canceled. I remember the email I received from one of the producers stating "I'm sure we will be able to reschedule the audition towards the end of the month". I certainly agreed, but as it turns out rarely have I ever been that wrong in my entire life. It was such a crazy time. I just had signed a 15 month lease for $3000.00 a month on March 1st and then, bam, just like that everything changed. I was in shock. Everyone in downtown Los

Angeles was walking around outside with masks on and unfortunately because of misinformation and scare tactics by the government many still do. I felt like I was cast in a movie I didn't want to be in. I kept thinking things would turn around, but instead everything just kept getting worse. I think for me the biggest shock was when the NBA canceled the remainder of their season. Never in my life did I think the world could stop like this. I never questioned the fact that Covid was real, but I knew right from the start the whole truth was not being told. The first thing that bothered me was the way information was and still is being controlled and censored. Any doctor who disagreed with the narrative that was being fed to us by our government was called a conspiracy theorist or an out and out liar. Many were threatened and lost their jobs. The government taking this stance should have sent the bat signal out to everyone that something is wrong here, but due to their fear most Americans went along without so much as a single question. I couldn't believe how easily everyone just gave up every single freedom they had and listened to a government who has never done anything but lie to them. People love to be told what to do I guess. The draconian measures that Anthony Fauci called for have had endless amounts of negative consequences and those consequences will continue to be felt for years to come. Almost nothing that Fauci and our government did was based on science yet that was their mantra the entire time. "Follow the science", was repeated daily, but science was never guiding us through the pandemic at all. I feel like I'm going to start rambling here and let some of my emotions take over because it's difficult to convey how angry I am with all you fools who obeyed your government and tried to shame and blame anyone who actually questioned things that didn't make sense. I will start with a Covid timeline and then get into some of the governmental contradictions, lies and nefarious acts. The CDC and the Department of Defense's timelines are both long and boring so I will try to keep this much shorter. If you would like to see either timeline for the CDC's timeline go to cdc.gov and search for David J. Sencer CDC Museum: In Association with the Smithsonian Institution. For the Department of Defenses timeline you can go to www.defense.gov/Spotlights/Coronavirus-DOD-Response/Timeline/

In December of 2019 a group of individuals in Wuhan, China became sick and the illness did not respond to standard treatments. At the time no one in China's government or any other official organization was calling this Covid. However, looking back you would think this might have been the first indication that this virus may have come from the Wuhan lab. However, that theory was immediately shut down because Dr. Fauci and the National Institute of Health were providing funding to the Wuhan Institute of Virology to perform gain of function research so they didn't want to be blamed for creating the virus that started the pandemic and killed millions. Dr. Fauci lied to Congress when he stated that the NIH "has not ever and does not now fund gain of function research in the Wuhan Institute of Virology" but more on that later. Even to this day the official narrative is that the virus was not started at the Wuhan lab, but we now know that is a complete, bullshit, lie. Most scientists who are free to share the truth in which they believe feel that it more than likely came from the Wuhan Institute and various agencies have also concluded the virus more than likely originated from the Wuhan lab.. John Stewart called out their bullshit on the Colbert Show when he said "the disease is the same name as the lab!". The whole interview was very funny and in large part because he pointed out the obvious! Of course it was made in the lab that works on novel corrona viruses and coincidentally is right where the pandemic started. Oh, but because Stewart went against his team's narrative the insults flew like pies in an old vaudeville show. A tweet storm ensued calling Stewart a conspiracy theorist and long time fans questioning his intelligence and is Stewart all of the sudden a right wing nut job. The stupidity of the masses will never cease to amaze me. Follow your team unquestionably all the way no matter the consequences. Everyone chooses a side and riding with that side no matter what is one of the main problems nowadays. Everyone picks a side and the truth means nothing unless it comes out of their chosen side's mouths.

On December 31st, 2019 the World Health Organization was officially informed of several additional cases of pneumonia with symptoms ranging from a fever, to shortness of breath and a severe cough. China's official narrative was established at this time when China determined the cases seem to be connected to the Huanan Seafood Wholesale Market. Due to this connection the Chinese government shuts down the Huanan Seafood Wholesale Market on January 1st 2020. Happy New Year everyone! Things started moving fast now and on January 2nd the WHO activated their Incident Management Support Team and cases rose rapidly.

January 7th 2020 is the day the virus went from an "unknown" cause of illness to the novel coronavirus being named as the causative agent. Although the WHO did not make their announcement until January 10th 2020. The virus is not contained in China and on Jan 13th Thailand became the first country outside of China to report a coronavirus case.

January 20th 2020 the first case of coronavirus is noted in the United States from a January 18th lab sample taken in Washington State.

January 31st 2020 the WHO declares the 2019 Novel Coronavirus a Public Health Emergency of International Concern. Also Alex Azar the Secretary of the Department of Health and Human Services declares the coronavirus a public health emergency.

February 4th 2020 the FDA approves the SARS-CoV-2 diagnostic test kit. Testing was certainly needed, but presently Covid testing is just a source of income for these companies that now have influence in government and they don't want to stop their flow of government money. If you are sick, stay home, it doesn't matter if it's covid, the flu, or the common cold. If you're sick, keep your sick ass home and stop spreading your germs.

February 25th 2020 the CDC's incident manager for the Covid 19 response holds a telebriefing and informs the nation to expect efforts to control the spread of Covid to include school closings, workplace shutdowns, and the canceling of large gatherings and public events.

February 29th 2020 the first death from Covid 19 is reported in the United States by the CDC and the Washington Department of Public Health.

March 6th 2020 President Trump signs an $8.3 billion dollar Covid 19 response bill for non Department of Defense relief.

March 10th 2020 the Department of Defense issues Force Health Protection Guidance (Supplement 3). Two items should be noted here and are of serious importance.

1.Respirators, including N95 filtering facepiece devices. These items are not recommended for use outside of healthcare settings.

2. Surgical masks and other facemasks. These items are intended to reduce the spread of viruses when worn by those known or suspected to be infected. Wearing a surgical mask does not provide respiratory protection to individuals who are not infected.

I think all of us who aren't in the current Fauci/CNN/MSNBC/Big Pharma/ U.S. Government bubble all remember Anthony Fauci stating "there's no reason to be walking around with a mask.' It's honestly hilarious that as I was reading various articles on various sites about this topic every site on the left either out and out lies and say's Fauci never said the aforementioned direct quote from that little lying weasel's mouth or they give the old "yes but" explanation. I really dislike that little lying elf looking fucker.

March 11th, 2020 The World Health Organization officially declares Covid 19 a pandemic. Also on March 11th, 2020 the United States enacted travel restrictions from Europe which began March 13th for 30 days. *Here is where things quickly go from bad to worse.

March 15th, 2020 States began to enact massive shutdowns in hope of preventing the further spread of Covid. Spoiler alert; it didn't work.

March 19th, 2020 Gavin Newsom issued a statewide stay at home order and the California governor shut down all non essential businesses. Of course the rules Gavin made never applied to himself, his family or his business. The California governor shut down wineries in 19 counties due to Covid 19, but kept his own tasting room in the Napa Valley open.

March 27th, 2020 President Trump signed the Coronavirus Aid, Relief and Economic Security Act. The CARES Act offers small business loans, loans to large industries and corporations, funding to state and local governments as well as $1200.00 payments for adults and additional funds for families with children.

April 30th, 2020 President Trump announces 'Operation Warp Speed' which was an attempt to create a vaccine against Covid in unprecedented time. The program funds the development of six potential vaccines.

July 23rd, 2020 The U.S. reaches 4 million confirmed Covid Cases. Of course with so many individuals being asymptomatic the number was probably much higher.

July 29th, 2020 Deaths related to Covid soars to over 150,000 but that number is misleading and we will never know the true Covid death numbers because if an individual was dying of some other cause and then they also contracted Covid the official cause of death was listed as Covid. CNN shockingly allowed Dr. Leana Wen to admit the fact that early on Covid deaths were probably counted more correctly with the majority of deaths listed as 'Covid deaths' where Covid was the primary cause. Dr. Wen states that it has probably shifted and we need to have three classifications; 1. Covid primary cause. 2. Secondary cause. 3. Covid as an incidental cause. On a sad note the higher ups at CNN probably spoke to her after the show and informed Dr. Wen if she would like to continue coming on the show she better not contribute to those 'Covid Conspracy's'. Also, the left lost their minds after she made these truthful statements. Anything that goes against the narrative that side has been fed is of course nothing but a lie and now someone that they loved listening to is being called a "conspiracy theorist" etc.

August 8th, 2020 President Trump signs memorandums providing assistance to homeowners and renters, deferring payroll tax obligations, and extending student loan payment relief through the end of the 2020. See, even Trump isn't all bad. I still didn't or don't like Mr. Trump, but he was unintentionally really funny at times. Especially when he whooped Hillary after Hillary and the Dems stole the primaries from Bernie.

June 29th, 2020 Gilead Sciences who received approximately 6.5 billion dollars in public funding will charge $3,120.00 for its drug Remdesivir. This will be a recurring theme by all drug companies who profited off the taxpayers dollars in creating vaccines, therapeutics etc. It really is a great example of how corporations benefit and use socialism to make money, fund projects etc., but then as soon as they can turn a profit it's Capitalism all the way baby.

July 14th, 2020 the CDC calls on everyone to wear cloth face masks when leaving their homes to prevent the spread of Covid 19 even though cloth masks don't protect you against Covid-19, but I guess it makes the idiot masses feel safe. What the CDC should have done along with the news organizations and the government is tell people the single best thing they could do to protect themselves against Covid and assure better outcomes was to eat healthy. exercise and lose weight. Unfortunately that step was never taken. Instead the government pushed everyone to wear a mask that does nothing, and to get vaccinated, which appears not be near the help the government and the pharmaceutical companies said it would be.

August 11th, 2020 the Trump administration agrees to pay $15.00 dollars per dose to Moderna for 100 million doses of the Covid -19 vaccine which amounted to $1.5 billion dollars and helped keep the fulfillment of governments number one job; to transfer public funds to corporations.

June 25th, 2023 which is the day I was writing this and getting extremely bored with this timeline so I am sure you are as well. I promise I am trying to limit this as much as possible, but I will try to skip ahead and bring this to an end before we both lose our minds or have PTSD from reliving this Covid nightmare. As I'm reading through the Defense Department and the CDC's time lines it's blowing my mind how every couple of days I read "Department of Defense in coordination with the Department of Health and Human Services awards $139.3M contract to" then insert various companies names and dollar amounts. The money for testing companies alone is insane. No wonder why in downtown Los Angeles I still see testing sites everywhere. No one wants to shut off these money spickets.

September 16th, 2020 HHS announces free Covid 19 vaccines for all my U.S. friends! (Just to be clear, nothing is free) After paying for research and development taxpayers will now have to pony up to vaccinate as many people as possible.

October 2nd, 2020 President Trump tests positive for Covid. Now if this overweight, non healthy, non exercising, big mac and french fry eating fucker can survive Covid that should have given everyone hope.

February 27th, 2021 The FDA approves an emergency use authorization for Johnson & Johnson's Covid 19 vaccine for all individuals 18 years and older.

March 8th, 2021 The CDC states that people who are fully vaccinated can safely gather with other fully vaccinated individuals indoors without the use of masks or social distancing. This is when the government really started trying to seperate the vaccinated vs. the unvaccinated even though a vaccinated person could still both get and spread Covid. Therefore there is no difference between a vaccinated person and an unvaccinated person except to the individual who was either vaccinated or unvaccinated. My family actually was going to have a "Vaccinated Only" Christmas Eve gathering. The thought of this made me so angry at the time and still absolutely sickens me. I just can't for the life of me understand how people fell so easily for government propaganda and they still have no clue! My blood is currently boiling as I am writing this.

March 11th 2021 President Biden signs the 1.9 trillion dollar American Rescue Plan into law.

This next sequence is a little strange, maybe?

March 14th 2021 Ireland, Iceland, Denmark and Norway suspended AstraZeneca's Covid 19 vaccine due to possible blood clot issues.

March 18th, 2021 The U.S. announces it will send 4 million doses of AstraZeneca's Covid 19 vaccine to Mexico and Canada. Both countries are like "wait, what?? AstraZeneca's??"

May 10th 2021 The FDA expands emergency use authorization for the Pfizer BioNTech Covid vaccine to ages 12-15 years old even though kids have almost no risks when getting Covid and usually do not even show symptoms.

May 13th The Deputy Secretary of Defense removes the requirement for masks, but only for fully vaccinated individuals. This is another step by the government to attempt to create two separate societies. The vaccinated vs. the unvaccinated even though again since both groups can both get and spread Covid there is only a difference for the individual who is vaccinated or not vaccinated, not society on the whole. You dumb, fucking assholes!!!

June 1st, 2021 The Delta variant is first identified in India and becomes the dominant variant in the United States. The media went crazy every time a new variant was discovered and continually used scare tactics in order to keep everyone on high fear alert. What they should have been saying is this is great news because as viruses mutate they become weaker and more spreadable. So is it the vaccine that's keeping people out of the hospital or is it the weaker variant combined with the variant spreading like wildfire and boosting the population's natural immunity? It's a valid question, but one that will never be asked by the mainstream, corporate media or by our government.

June 2nd, 2021 President Biden announces a national month of action to encourage all Americans to get vaccinated by July 4th. The propaganda is insane and all to transfer your tax dollars to all the industries that are continuing to benefit from all our Covid policies, especially the pharmaceutical industry with the pushing of the vaccines.

June 10th, 2021 President Biden announces the United States will purchase and donate a half a billion Pfizer vaccines and donate them to middle income countries and Africa. More American generosity right? Our generosity is almost always to enrich our corporations even more than they already are. So these vaccines that were funded with our tax dollars are now purchased with our tax dollars and given somewhere like the continent of Africa that has never had a Covid problem and whose people pay Covid no attention and don't want to take the vaccine because it's not needed. Who knows, maybe the continent of Africa has done so well with Covid because Africa's obesity rate is approximately 18% for women and 7% for men, whereas America has an obesity rate closing in on 50%.

June 15, 2021 The United States exceeds 600,000 Covid 19 "related" deaths. You know why I put "related" in quotes so don't pretend you don't.

June 25th, 2021 The Biden Administration announces the United States will donate 3 million doses of the Johnson & Johnson vaccine to Afghanistan. The good news is Afghanistan will have better protection against Covid. The bad news is the vaccines provide no protection against U.S. bombs being dropped on your heads.

November 8th, 2021 All non U.S. citizens will be required to be fully vaccinated in order to fly into the United States. All passengers will also need to show a negative pre departure Covid 19 test. The latter should have been the only requirement. The crazy thing is the U.S. still has this insane policy that you have to be vaccinated in order to enter our country. Why is it that facts mean nothing!? It does not matter to society on the whole if someone is vaccinated or not. This ridiculous policy prevented Novak Djokovic from playing in the U.S. Open. Djokovic is one of the most fit athletes in the world, but you want him to inject something into his body that he doesn't need to show our control. Oh, and shame on all those who bashed Djokovic. Individuals like ESPN's Micheal Wilbon, who I get it, you're a fat, lazy out of shape bastard that needs the vaccine, but Novak Djokovic isn't so guess what Micheal Wilbon, you should shut the fuck up.

November 19th, 2021 The CDC urges everyone 18 years and older should receive a booster. Of course they did.

December 20th The CDC releases data estimating the Omicron

variant is approximately 1.6 times more transmissible than the Delta variant. Yes, assholes, again with each mutation the virus becomes more transmissible and weaker. The CDC, the WHO, the government and the media all seem to leave the second part of that equation out for some reason though. Hmmm, I'm pretty sure it's to keep their followers in fear and eager to comply with whatever the government tells them to do.

January 19th, 2022 The Biden Administration purchases 1 billion additional tests and creates an online portal so people can get Covid 19 tests sent to them for "free".

April 29th, 2022 The CDC estimates that as of February 2022 75% of children and adolescents have Covid antibodies proving that a vaccine is not necessary for most children and adolescents.

May 31st, 2022 The U.S.Department of Justice asks a federal judge to overturn the April 18th order from a Florida judge declaring the CDC's mandate requiring individuals to wear a mask on public transportation because God forbid anyone go against what the government tells them to do.

June 18, 2022 The CDC recommends Covid 19 vaccines for young children aged 6 months through 5 years of age. So that completes it. Now the CDC wants everyone vaccinated regardless of any risk vs. reward consideration. Oh wait, they did give you 6 months after the baby came into the world.

December 8th 2022 The FDA finally followed the CDC and also recommended Covid 19 vaccines for children down to 6 months of age, leaving out the precious newborns.

The Great Barrington Declaration

The Great Barrington Declaration was written in October of 2020 in response to the United States following the actions of China and many other countries throughout the world who were enacting fascist policies that would have lasting physical and mental health consequences. The declaration recommended an approach the authors referred to as "Focused Protection".

"The most compassionate approach that balances the risks and benefits of reaching herd immunity, is to allow those who are at minimum risk of death to live their lives normally to build up immunity to the virus through natural infection, while better protecting those who are at higher risk." The declaration gives an example of what protecting the vulnerable would look like in nursing homes, but left that implementation along with other scenarios up to public health officials.

The declaration went on to state "Those who are not vulnerable should immediately be allowed to resume life as normal. Simple hygiene measures, such as hand washing and staying home when sick should be practiced by everyone to reduce the herd immunity threshold. Schools and universities should be open for in-person teaching. Extracurricular activities such as sports, should be resumed. Young low-risk adults should work normally, rather than from home. Restaurants and other businesses should open. Arts, music, sport and other cultural activities should resume. People who are more at risk may participate if they wish, while society as a whole enjoys the protection conferred upon the vulnerable by those who have built up herd immunity. The Great Barrington Declaration was written and signed by;

Dr. Martin Kulldorff, professor of medicine at Harvard University, a biostatistician, and epidemiologist with expertise in detecting and monitoring infectious disease outbreaks and vaccine safety evaluations.

Dr. Sunetra Gupta, professor at Oxford University, an epidemiologist with expertise in immunology, vaccine development, and mathematical modeling of infectious diseases.

Dr. Jay Bhattacharya, professor at Stanford University Medical School, a physician, epidemiologist, health economist, and public health policy expert focusing on infectious diseases and vulnerable populations.

The Great Barrington Declaration was later signed and endorsed by thousands of epidemiologists, physicians, and medical and public health scientists. As the declaration gained momentum and popularity the powers that be decided they needed to attack and kill this strategy as it did not fit into their lockdown agenda. In emails between Dr. Fauci and Dr. Francis Collins who was the director of the National Institutes of Health, the two strategize and apparently used the media to discredit the Great Barrington Declaration so that the common sense strategy that would have helped millions would not prevail. In Collins's October 8th, 2020 email to Fauci, Collins writes "This proposal from the three fringe epidemiologists... seems to be getting a lot of attention - and even a co-signature from Nobel Prize winner Mike Leavitt at Stanford. Dr. Collins writes to Dr. Fauci "There needs to be a quick and devastating published take down of its premises. Is it underway?" I'm so disgusted by this email. I think about all we have been through as a country and how much better all our lives would have been if we followed the Great Barrington Declaration (GBD) strategy. Protect the most vulnerable and the rest of us should have been left with choices. The government and private corporations took away our freedom, and our free will. It's difficult to imagine this was even possible at such a massive level. Making sure efforts were underway to delegitimize GBD in an interview with the Washington Post Dr. Collins stated "This is a fringe component of epidemiology. This is not mainstream science. It's dangerous." Yeah, it's dangerous to their "lock us down, and vaccinate us all" mandates. The government made sure Facebook posts, and Twitter tweets mentioning the GBD were taken down. The government even went so far as to have Google deboost the Great Barrington Declaration so that if anyone searched for the GBD the declaration would be hidden so far down in the results no one could find it and what the search would produce was all negative articles about the GBD. That bullshit was repeated even on sites such as Reddit and scientific debate was squashed everywhere. Perhaps if 'Focused Protection" were followed the outcomes would have been much better. Not only individuals mental health, and all other aspects of our health, but perhaps even the death toll could have been smaller. According to the New York Times the total Covid deaths in the United States was 1.12 million and counting. The United States with all its strict lockdown protocols ended up being number one in Covid deaths. Well, at least we are finally legitimately number one at something. Had Andrew Cuomo, the initial darling of the pandemic with his talks with his brother Chris on CNN followed the GBD's recommendation of protecting the most vulnerable perhaps NYS would not have had completely botched the way they handled dealing with nursing homes. More than 12% of New York State's long term care population died from Covid-19.

Had the Great Barrington Declaration been implemented that number could have been much less. We have to take into account that many of the Covid deaths are 'Covid-19 related' deaths. Covid related means that could have had cancer, heart disease, diabetes, kidney failure, etc., all medical issues that due to lockdowns and fear mongering people failed to get treatment for. If we would have focused on the most vulnerable and had the media's narrative been of that then people would not have been so deathly afraid when they were never in a risk category to die of Covid in the first place. They brainwashed so many people, especially young people who literally have almost zero risk from Covid especially since Covid has mutated into the weaker strains. The GBD is what we should have followed and if Covid is around for two more years or a two hundred more years or if there is another pandemic in the future The Great Barrington Declaration is the best strategy and is what we will need to implement.

Failed Government Policies

As State and Federal government interventions began I was again in utter disbelief. Here I was in a new State, a new apartment, a new life where I didn't know anyone and had zero social support and I was basically locked in my apartment. I'm sure many people had it much worse than I did so I don't want to make it sound insanely bad, I'm just laying out what I was thinking and feeling. At the apartment I lived in they shut down the pool area and the recreation room where I would go and shoot some pool so I didn't have anywhere to go to entertain myself. Thank the Lord for streaming services though because there was a lot of television watching going on. The city of Los Angeles and Southern California in general completely changed.

When I first got here most people were very friendly and social and then once Covid hit people wouldn't even look at you much less get within 6 feet of you. I have been at the corner waiting for a light to change and the person who was approximately 6 feet away and wearing a mask would literally run away from me because I wasn't wearing a mask outside. Los Angeles seemed exceptionally soft when it came to Covid and Los Angeles still is extremely soft to this very day when it comes to Covid. I consider myself to be someone who is politically way to the left and as part of that mindset I believe personal freedom is a cornerstone of being on the left, but for many reasons that was not the case with Covid. The side that knows the government does nothing but lie suddenly was eating everything the government was feeding them without question.

In Los Angeles I also think because the media tried to put all anti government Covid policy people in the Trump camp, people here were afraid of being looked at as a Trump supporter. Of course that is far from the truth and I've noticed many of the Bernie Sanders supporters turned out to be people who were able to think for themselves, knew you can't trust the government and big Pharma and so we have questioned everything that seemed to need questioning and as it turned out we were right about everything! Los Angeles is a different animal though and as I mentioned previously so many people here are still walking around outside by themselves wearing a mask.

There is no science behind their fear and it shows the government how easily they can be controlled which I believe is some of the reason for many of these restrictive policies. Governments eliminated large gatherings including sporting events. Never in my life did I think NBA, NHL, MLB and NFL games along with every other sport could be canceled. I thought there is way too much money in sports to have them canceled. Damn, I wish I could have been right. When sporting events finally did open back up it was hilarious seeing how angry people got who didn't want any kind of normal life to be lived ever again. All nonessential businesses were forced to close including gyms, salons, bars, shops, restaurants, which crushed almost every small business you could think of. People who owned a family business their entire life lost everything and the government barely seemed to care. If the government shuts down a business that generates $10,000.00 a month then the government should have had to pay those business owners $10,000.00 a month.

Parks were even closed and individuals who were seen at a park were harassed and kicked out by the police. Parks should have never been closed. That would have been one giant step in the right direction and could have allowed people to exercise and socialize safely and spared so many of some of the mental anguish they had to endure. The government has seemed to get everything wrong at every turn throughout this pandemic. Many states required masks to be worn even if social distancing could be observed. So many of the restrictions came and went as Covid numbers rose and fell. This never made any sense to me because we were never going to get to zero. Numbers would fall then the government would relax restrictions and the Covid numbers would rise again causing the government to react and re-implement the restrictions again. My issue was who cares if numbers rise and fall. As long as you are healthy you weren't and still aren't going to end up in the hospital. Let everyone get Covid and build a strong natural immunity. Protect the vulnerable and let everyone else live their lives. Once the virus mutated and became more spreadable it was obvious almost everyone was going to ge Covid at some point. I have family members who were super careful, hardly left the house and certainly didn't go anywhere without a mask and they ended up getting Covid just as I did. As businesses throughout the country shut down people suffered. The government did some good things with opening unemployment benefits and adding a federal contribution to what the states were giving. However, if you had a job that relied on tips you were in serious trouble. I personally know many individuals who worked in the service area in states like Arizona where unemployment benefits were low, those people no longer had enough money to pay their rent and buy food.

The Fed cut interest rates to range from 0% to 0,25%. The Fed kept the rates low but as employment rates recovered and inflation rose above the Fed's 2% target by the end of 2021 the Fed signaled they would raise interest rates in 2022. Now as we are into 2023 and inflation is through the roof the Fed is trying to get a handle on inflation and as prices come down slowly they will eventually stop raising interest rates. Of course for much of the economy inflation is nothing more than an excuse for greedy corporations to raise prices and make record profits. The whole choosing a side thing comes in big time with inflation. Those on the right all blame Biden and even though I can't stand President Biden, inflation is nothing more than corporate greed. You can't have companies making record profits and then blame higher prices on inflation so those on the right blame Biden and politicians of the left stay silent because they refuse to call out their corporate owners.

The Biden administration shamefully and more than likely at the behest of the pharmaceutical industry used authoritative measures to force millions to be vaccinated. President Biden mandated that all companies with more than 100 workers require vaccination. Biden also mandated vaccinations for all health care workers, federal contractors and federal workers, and anyone who exercised their rights to body autonomy were warned they would face disciplinary actions. What are you, our father? Biden went on to chastise the unvaccinated by stating, "we have been patient, but our patience is wearing thin. And your refusal has cost all of us." Biden went on to incorrectly state "We need to protect vaccinated workers from the unvaccinated." That's the kind of bullshit rhetoric that had all the brainwashed idiots around the country thinking one person's vaccination status affects another person. For the 100th time! Both vaccinated and unvaccinated people can both get and spread Covid. Everyone on the vaccination side tried to do everything to make two separate societies. Going back to the NFL quickly, the NFL even forced non vaccinated people to wear a red wristband. Hello Nazi Germany. The Supreme Court did partially make the right decision when it ruled the Occupational Safety and Health Administration (OSHA) did not have the authority to force vaccinations onto the private sector but the Supreme Court did uphold the Centers for Medicare and Medicaid Services ability to force vaccines on employees at hospitals, nursing homes and health care providers that receive federal funds. Unfortunately, places like NYC ignored the Supreme Court's ruling and still tried to enforce some of the strictest vaccination policies in the nation. Shame on Bill de Blasio, and shame on President Biden. Both were working for those who would profit off these mandates and that's why there's no way I will support Biden as he attempts to secure a second term.

The government's mask mandates and closing of businesses hurt the economy and individuals' health to spite whatever economic decisions were made by the Fed and whatever help the State and the Federal government tried to give. The mask mandates and closing of businesses, and schools did not seem to have helped curve the spread of Covid and certainly were not worth the costs we paid in every other aspect of our lives. States like Florida and Texas in many ways fared better with their non restrictive policies than States like California and New York who were like Nazi Germany. New York had the second most deaths per capita only trailing New Jersey while Florida and Texas ranked 26th and 24th respectively. Many would make the argument that New York's population is much more dense resulting in the greater deaths, but many rural areas throughout the country had worse health results with Covid to spite being isolated. California did slightly better than both Florida and Texas coming in at 30th. However with many people in California not being treated for mental health disorders, which have skyrocketed, not getting cancer treatment, or tested for other various diseases etc. and as the death rates rise from all of those diseases over the next few years I think it is going to be crystal clear the strict policies of New York and California were not the way to go.

Forced Vaccination

To me this was about as UnAmerican and corrosive as things could possibly get. The U.S. government at the behest of the pharmaceutical industry tried desperately to force people to choose between feeding their families or having the right to choose what they put in their own bodies. I know so many people who did not want to get the vaccine, but it was either get the vaccine or lose the job you've been working at for the last 20+

years. They were in an impossible situation. Many of those people were married with kids so they were forced to make a choice that would affect their families. I'm not talking about affecting them in the bullshit way the government and pharma said not taking the vaccine would affect others, but the choice of not getting vaccinated or losing your job truly does affect your family. It's disgusting because there was no scientific reason to force any healthy individual to get vaccinated. Being overweight was the number one determining factor as to how well you would do if you got Covid, but the government didn't force you to stop eating McDonald's or ice cream and exercise did they? Shit, the government and the media wouldn't even dare suggest those options.

As I mentioned earlier professional athletes were forced to get the vaccine and there is absolutely no reason for a professional athlete who are all fairly young and in fantastic physical shape to get vaccinated. The few athletes that were able to think for themselves were punished and harassed for refusing to get vaccinated just as the rest of us were. We were all called "anti-vaxxers" even though we aren't anti vaccine, we are just anti this untested, unproven vaccine. A typical vaccine development timeline takes somewhere between 5 and 10 years. However The FDA issued an emergency use authorization bypassing the usual safety measures only time allows for. The Buffalo Bills's Cole Beasley continuously was verbally attacked by fans, media and punished by the NFL for not being vaccinated. Mr. Beasley stood up to the NFL and the players union by refusing to get vaccinated and then calling the NFL out when Covid-19 protocols were changed for vaccinated players, but kept in place for unvaccinated players. I'm not sure how stupid people have to be to not understand there is no difference between a vaccinated person and an unvaccinated person any more than there is a difference because of the color of your skin! Both parties can get and spread Covid! I know I've mentioned this before and probably will mention it again because it infuriates me that so many policies were put in place based on there being a difference and so many individuals also thought and still think there is a difference. So why were the powers that be trying to separate the two groups? It was in part to punish those who dare not listen and do what their government tells them to do! This is all a huge transfer of funds from the U.S. population to the vaccine makers, and the many other companies that benefit from Covid. The government is now allowing insurance companies to incentivise parents to get their kids vaccinated by paying them. A friend of mine was paid $50.00 per kid to have her children vaccinated. So, breaking this down; We paid for the research and development of a vaccine, then we purchased the vaccine back from the pharmaceutical companies and now we are giving insurance companies money to give to individuals so they will get their children vaccinated at no cost to them. We are all paying every step of the way and it's just transferring more of our money to those companies like Pfizer, Moderna, Johnson & Johnson, AstraZeneca and many more.

Unvaccinated NFL players had to be tested daily and were heavily restricted in locker rooms, team hotels, and the cafeteria. Unvaccinated players also had to adhere to social distancing standards that vaccinated players did not have to. As with most rules that were applied during the pandemic there was zero science behind these NFL protocols since both the vaccinated and unvaccinated could both get and spread Covid equally. I loved this one meme that stated "Sorry, we prefer to catch Covid from vaccinated people". Many athletes paid a financial and social price for having the audacity to choose what they put or don't put into their own bodies. As I mentioned earlier, one of my favorite tennis players of all time, Novak Djokovic, refused to get vaccinated. Djokovic who is a nine time Australian Open champion and who is attempting to prove he is the greatest tennis player of all time made a choice that cost him being able to play in tournaments in what many would consider the waning years of his prime. Djokovic was forced to miss multiple grand slam tournaments due to his unvaccinated status after coming off a year in 2021 where he won the Australian Open, French Open, and Wimbledon. It's a shame and Djokovic was unable to play in this year's U.S. Open because even though restrictions have been loosened the U.S. still requires foreigners to be vaccinated in order to enter the country. You would think a negative Covid test would be more important than your vaccination status, but because common sense is nowhere to be found when it comes to all the Covid policy nonsense that is not the case. Finally, as of May 11th, 2023 the U.S. no longer requires proof of vaccination for foreign travelers.

Some other amazing athletes that I truly respect for standing their ground regardless of the consequences are NBA star Jonathan Isaac who stated "I am not anti-vax, I'm not anti medicine, I am not anti-science, but with that being said, it is my belief that the vaccine status of every person should be their own choice. Completely up to them without bullying, without being pressured, without being forced into doing so." Well said Mr. Isaac.

Another NBA player who I respected so much for exercising his choice as to what he puts in his own body was NBA superstar Kyrie Irving. The seven time NBA all star who was recently traded to the Dallas Mavericks paid a costly financial price along with getting torched daily by a media who tried to bully Mr. Irving every step of the way. Everyone from that ignorant, out of shape loudmouth Micheal Wilbon, to Steven A. Smith, and numerous others who now looking back were all dead wrong and owe Kyrie an apology that I'm certain he will not get. As a matter of fact the only ESPN analyst who shared any common sense and intelligence during this whole Covid crisis was Jay Williams. It's crazy to say, but in speaking out Mr. Williams was actually brave because at the time it seemed as if he might have been putting his own job on the line. Williams stated "The media is a problem. The fear mongering needs to stop. Every damn narrative I read over the past couple of days… is the unvaxxed vs the vaxxed. The minorities voice that shouldn't be heard, the progressive NBA is not setting the right example!" Some idiots in the media were still sticking to the narrative that Kyrie's choice to not be vaccinated was "killing others". No, no it wasn't you morons! The ignorance on the 'everyone must be vaccinated side' is mind blowing. Kyrie has integrity, something vaccine bullies lacked. Kyrie cost himself millions of dollars in order to take a stand on something he felt was important and something he knew he was right about.

Although I am not a golf fan I am now a fan of eighth time PGA tour champion Bryson DeChambeau. Bryson stated "I'm a healthy, young individual that will continue to work on my health." Hmmm, maybe something most everyone should have done during the pandemic.

Another high profile athlete along the lines of Kyrie Irving who remained unvaccinated was one of the greatest quarterbacks to ever walk on an NFL field, Mr. Aaron Rodgers. Rodgers was ambiguous about his vaccination status early on and honestly that's the only thing he did that I didn't agree with when it came to his stance on the Covid-19 vaccines. I think I understand why he was less than forthcoming on his vaccination status though. In my opinion Rodgers wasn't forthcoming about his vaccination status because he understood he would non stop be bullied and harassed by the NFL and the media. For that reason Rodgers chose to say he was "Immunized" basically hoping to trick the media. If I were him and any other player I would have come out and said "look, I am a professional athlete and I am in great physical condition. I don't feel Covid poses a serious risk to my health and I don't want to inject something in my body that is untested and we don't know if there are going to be any long term side effects. Furthermore since both vaccinated and unvaccinated players can both get and spread Covid I am not putting my teammates or anyone else in danger therefore it's no one's business, but mine as to what I decide to put into my body." I wish all the athletes would have been more vocal about why it's no one's business and that their vaccination status doesn't affect anyone but themselves!

As I've been trying to research information for this Covid chapter I have found it's impossible to find specific information that goes against what the government's agenda/position has been on Covid. All the powers that be including the government, the media, and the pharmaceutical industry have all controlled the narrative and continue to do so. I'm trying to find certain information about the Aarron Rodgers vaccination saga and after numerous attempts to change my wording and ask the question in different ways these are some of the headlines that came up; "Aaron Rodgers Somehow Sinks Even Lower", "Unvaccinated dumbass loser Aaron Rodgers", "Aaron Rodgers Whining Once Again about Covid and Biden", and "Kareem Abdul-Jabber Blasts Aaron Rodgers Anti-Vaccine" The reason I mention this is because it shows how difficult it is to find the truth in this Covid mess. Also, where are the apologies to these brave athletes? They were right about everything, and now as young athletes are dropping dead from cardiac arrest throughout the world, maybe everyone who is paying attention and took the vaccine is wishing they had not.

As a matter of fact not only do Aaron Rodgers and all the other athletes deserve an apology, but myself and everyone else who has been harassed by their family members and friends all deserve apologies. I know we wont get an apology because most people on the vaccination side are still unaware they were wrong and they don't want to see what horrible human beings they were over the course of the pandemic. Screaming "do what we say!!!" No, fuck you, you do what you want and I'll do what I feel is best for myself. I have a fantastic family and I know they are really great people who will do anything for their other family members. However because Covid was so politicized almost no one searched for the truth and if they didn't hear it from their side it didn't matter. My family always gets together on Thanksgiving, and Christmas Eve. There are probably 50 to 60 of us and we have been doing this for 50+ years, but after the vaccinations came out those who were vaccinated thought they might have a "vaccinated only" Thanksgiving. I have to say, I was furious. Why the hell can't people get it through their heads? It does not matter if you are vaccinated or unvaccinated! Both vaxed and unvaxed get and spread Covid! So stop it! I know my family was and some still are just brainwashed. It's funny because I couldn't stand Trump and something I didn't like about those who were Trump supporters was if they didn't hear something from Trump or Fox news then it wasn't true. Now the situation is reversed and the 'vaccinate everyone' crowd turned into the exact thing I didn't like about many Trump supporters.. If Fauci or CNN, MSNBC etc. didn't say it then it is not true. The truth means nothing to most people unless it comes from the side they are already on.

Fauci Emails and Deposition

In my opinion Dr. Fauci was the single most influential and destructive figure throughout the pandemic. Hopefully as the truth slowly comes out Dr. Fauci will go down as one of the most destructive people in the history of the United States. Dr. Fauci labeled himself as the all knowing expert and if any other scientist or doctor had a difference of opinion then Dr. Fauci used his platform and his power and ensured the theory at odds with

Fauci's own would be discredited and stomped out on social media so it could never gain any mainstream consciousness. Dr. Fauci seemed to truly enjoy his newfound fame and went on every television and youtube program he could fit into his schedule. Dr. Fauci used the spotlight to control the narrative and Fauci fear mongered every step of the way. When a new variant would arise Dr. Fauci would be all over the television warning about the dangers and emphasizing that we need to wear a mask, get vaccinated, and stay home by ourselves. Fauci also stated "most importantly to always wear a mask while driving in a car by yourself". Okay, Dr. Fauci may not have said that last part, but I'm sure Dr. Fauci was proud of all these idiots in their car by themselves wearing a mask because I guess you can't be too careful.

Anthony Fauci was deposed in the ***State of Missouri ex rel. Schmitt., et al. v. Joseph R Biden, Jr., et al,*** on November 23rd 2022. The questioning was led by Missouri Solicitor General John Sauer. Reading through Dr. Fauci's deposition was not fun. There were way too many set up questions that led to nothing but Dr. Fauci stating "I don't recall" time after time after time (174 times to be exact!). One question Dr. Fauci answered "I don't recall" was a question about a friend of Fauci named Sylvia Burwell. Sylvia Burwell is the former Secretary of the Department of Health and Human Services and the current President of American University. In February of 2020 Mrs. Burwell emailed Dr. Fauci and asked if she should wear a mask in an airport while traveling. When questioned about this email Dr. Fauci's response was "You know, I don't recall specifically that. I - - I do know that Sylvia has called me over the last couple of years asking me questions about health. I don't specifically recall that." Mr. Sauer then asked "Do you recall writing this in response: "Masks are really for infected people to prevent them from spreading infection to people who are not infected, rather than protecting uninfected people from acquiring infection. The typical mask you buy in the drugstore is not really effective in keeping out a virus, which is small enough to pass through material. It might, however, provide some slight benefit in keeping out gross droplets if someone coughs or sneezes on you. I do not recommend that you wear a mask, particularly since you're going to a low risk location." Keep in mind when Dr. Fauci initially told the world on television that masks do not work he later stated he said that because he wanted to make sure there were enough masks in supply for medical workers and he was afraid the general public would buy the masks and leave medical staff in short supply. However, this is his friend, and it's one or two masks so certainly if he didn't believe this to be true he would have told his friend the truth and that she should protect herself and mask up. When Mr. Sauer follows up and asks "Do you specifically recall recommending that she not wear a mask as she's traveling" Dr. Fauci goes back to his old faithful "I don't recall"

Forgetful Fauci goes on to his next set of forgetfulness when asked about the origins of coronavirus and how some scientists which Dr. Fauci was corresponding with felt it looked as if Covid indeed had been created in a lab. Dr. Fauci stated the first time someone had brought the concern the virus had been manipulated was in a phone conversation with scientists Christian Anderson and Jeremy Farrar. On the call with Dr. Anderson and Dr. Farrar it was decided a larger group of scientists should look further into the possibility of the virus being manufactured. In a later email between Dr. Fauci and Dr. Anderson, Dr. Anderson refers to some of the scientists by first name and writes "Eddie, Bob, Mike and myself all find the genome inconsistent with expectations from evolutionary theory". Dr. Anderson also writes "the unusual features of the virus make up a really small part of the genome so one has to look really closely at all of the sequences to see that some of the features potentially look engineered".

Dr. Fauci then emails his principal deputy Hugh Auchinclose with an attachment Fauci referred to as "SARS Baric, Shi, et al., Nature Medicine.". In the email Dr. Fauci describes the article as a 'gain of function' article. When Mr. Sauer asks Dr. Fauci three follow up questions about the email including "Do you know why you attached that article to this email to Hugh, your principal deputy?" As usual all three times Dr. Fauci responds to the questions with "I don't recall". Dr. Fauci made it clear it was imperative that Dr. Fauci and his principal deputy have a conversation in the morning before the scheduled call with a larger group of evolutionary virologists. According to Dr. Fauci the reason for this call was because this was the first time "I had heard of what we may or may not be funding through EcoHealth and others, and I wanted to get a better scope of just what the terrain of what we were doing in collaboration with different scientists," I have to ask the reader this; Do you believe this is this is really the first time Dr. Fauci became aware he was funding gain of function research through EcoHealth? I'm pretty sure you can guess my opinion on the matter. This is all obviously really important to Dr. Fauci. His reputation is at stake here, and I'm sure Dr. Fauci didn't want a repeat of his Aides debacle. Also, Dr. Fauci could possibly get the blame for millions of deaths. When Mr. Sauer asked Dr. Fauci if he remembered calling Hugh that day, do you want to guess Dr. Fauci's answer? You may as well, I mean you don't get that many opportunities in life to guess at something so easy. Well, if you guessed "I don't recall " you would be right, oh and if you didn't well, if you didn't you probably can't even read so you have other things to worry about.

I think this was weighing pretty heavily on Dr. Fauci's mind, but when asked by Mr. Sauer ``Were you concerned at that time that the work that you had funded in China might have led to the creation of the coronavirus? The lying leprechaun stated "I wasn't concerned". Do you know when someone coughs and says "bullshit"? I'm doing that in my head right now. The next bunch of questions Mr. Sauer asked were all about sending the Nature Medicine article and all were answered with "I don't recall" For a guy who seems to pretend to know everything he has a pretty poor memory. If you read this deposition you would honestly be blown away at how many times "I don't recall" is stated by Dr. Fauci. Don't do that to yourself though, I promise you will be as miserable for torturing yourself as I currently am. I keep having to take breaks because I literally want to smash my ipad and computer. How this scumbag has any credibility is astounding.

Okay, full disclosure, the scientists who once believed the coronavirus looked as if it was not natural and created in a lab did conclude it was not. Meanwhile the Energy Department, the FBI and anyone with half a brain knows the virus originated from the Wuhan Lab. Pressure was more than likely put on the scientists to reach a conclusion that protected their fellow scientists and maybe even their livelihoods. There are a few clues in the deposition though. Emails between Jeremy Farrar and Fauci, the two agree this should all be kept "in total confidence." Fauci and Farrar did not want the fact that this virus may have come from a lab getting out, or being debated at all. The two did not want anyone to even be aware the issue was being debated amongst their group. Jeremy Farrar was also worried about people talking about the origins of the virus on social media. Mr. Sauer follows up Farrar's social media concerns with a question to Dr. Fauci. Mr. Sauer asks "Were you ever concerned about what people would be saying on social media about the origins of the virus?" Fauci answers "I'm concerned about, you know, there being misinformation or disinformation that would interfere with our trying to save the lives of people throughout the world, which happens when people spread false claims." Fauci didn't want any debate even among scientists let alone people he felt couldn't use their common sense to filter through their lies. Fauci, being concerned about "disinformation" being spread on social media, tells Farrar "It;s essential that we move quickly." Fauci also stated he wanted to get the WHO to convene. The WHO is far from an unbiased organization and I will get into who funds the WHO and why unfortunately when you follow the money you see you can't trust anyone in power. At this point there are multiple emails from Jeremy Farrar expressing concern about chatter on social media about the origins of the virus. Dr. Fauci also seems to share the concern and to me they are almost in a panic mood over this. In an email with Francis Collins and Jeremy Farrar, Fauci writes, "We really need to get the WHO moving on getting the convening started." Dr. Fauci really seemed to want to get the WHO on board with the narrative that was best for him and when asked why of course Dr. Fauci replies with "I don't recall" Oh Lord, come on! So, there is this unbelievably important matter, important to the world, important to you personally, but yet you don't remember why you would have wanted the WHO to get moving.

In case you aren't sure as of yet, Dr. Fauci is lying! It's never ending with the lies. Dr. Fauci is asked about a specific conversation in an email that he is both receiving and responding to but when asked about the subject matter within the email Dr. Fauci almost always responds with "I don't recall", "I don't know what he was referring to" etc. etc. etc. over and over and over. Unless you read the deposition it is almost hard to believe and it's maddening! Here is the person who put himself up as the all knowing czar and now he's playing senile and it is so disrespectful to all of humanity! I guess it's pretty clear I'm beyond disgusted with Fauci, his cronies and much of society for being just plain ignorant. Finally on 02-26-2023 some good news and truth came from one of our government agency's. The

Energy Department concluded that a "Lab leak is most likely the origin of the Covid pandemic." This was a change in the Energy Departments earlier positions so hopefully this is a slight shift in some aspects of the country being able to tell the truth.

Keep in mind as discussed earlier we could have gone with the common sense strategy laid out in the Great Barrington Declaration of protecting the vulnerable, but Dr. Collins and Dr. Fauci decided for all of us that wasn't the right strategy and I'll remind the reader that Dr. Collins wrote to Dr. Fauci stated "There needs to be a quick and devastating published takedown of the Great Barrington Declaration". Dr. Collins and Dr. Fauci were worried about the attention the GBD declaration was getting and that the GBD even had the signature of Nobel Prize winner Mike Levitt of Stanford. Dr Collins wrote and asked Dr. Fauci if the devastating take down of the GBD was "underway". When asked about this subject Dr. Fauci replied "I don't know what he meant." Let's use common sense and realize even if Dr. Fauci is one of your heroes that Dr. Fauci knew exactly what Dr. Collings meant because it was something that was obviously being coordinated. ("You got to coordinate" Mr. Jackson, Boomerang, starring Eddie Murphy)

In emails between Dr. Fauci, Francis Collins and Cliff Lane it appears this coordination was underway. In an email from Dr. Fauci with the subject line being "the Great Barrington Declaration", Dr. Fauci attached an article from Wired Magazine by Matt Reynolds where Fauci states "Francis, I'm pasting in below a piece from The Wire that debunks this theory, correct?" Dr. Collins responds with "Excellent". I can picture Dr. Collins rubbing his hands together with an evil smile while saying "excellent". When Dr. Fauci was asked if he knew author Matt Reynolds or if he had any communication with him before he published his article Dr. Fauci as usual states "I don't recall". What!?? You don't recall if you had communication with an author? Are you fucking serious? This is just insulting, you either did or you didn't. There is no "not recalling" if you did or didn't have communication with Mr. Reynolds.

In various emails Dr. Fauci was concerned about misinformation getting out to the public, but really what Dr. Fauci was concerned with information getting out that he disagreed with. Dr. Fauci's office had a communications team that dealt with social media and online sites such as Youtube over what they deemed as 'vaccine communications, more specifically the misinformation in vaccine communications. Again, this is an attempt to control what 'they' being Dr. Fauci etc. are deemed as 'misinformation'. Often there were scientific studies done, but if our Lord and Covid Savior Dr. Fauci disagreed with the study then it must be stopped and we the people can not be allowed to read and think for ourselves using common sense and our best judgment to decide what makes more sense.

The communications team even had emails with the White House's digital director Clarke Humphrey to take down an instagram account. The CDC's Catherine Jamal emailed two individuals at facebook about the effectiveness of Ivermectin or as far as the CDC was concerned the ineffectiveness of Ivermectin and the misinformation being spread on social media about Ivermectins effectiveness. The Food and Drug Administration put out warnings against using Ivermectin stating Ivermectin could cause serious harm, hospitalization, seizures, is highly toxic and could result in "coma and even death". You would think they would have never approved such a dangerous drug to begin with. Could everyone from Dr. Fauci on down really be worried about the dangerous effects of Ivermectin or could they have been pushing back because the pharmaceutical companies didn't want anyone using this safe and inexpensive drug. I'm not saying Ivermectin was the answer for Covid because there have been independent studies and although some have found Ivermectin to have some benefits, most have not.

On CNN's State of the Union Dr. Fauci was showed a clip of conservative author Alex Berenson speaking at the Conservative Political Action Conference (CPAC) where Mr. Berenson stated "The government was hoping that they could sort of sucker 90% of the population into getting vaccinated, and it isn't happening,". Dr. Fauci's response to the quote, along with the fact that the audience applauded was "It's horrifying". That's what Dr. Fauci thinks of anyone who doesn't agree with what he thinks should be done with your health. Fauci went on to say "it's almost frightening for people to say they don't want health officials to save their lives." Dr. Fauci thinks it's his job to force everyone to take an unproven vaccine whether they like it or not. No, Dr. Fauci, it's your job to advise people what you think is the best option for them, then it's each individual's job to decide for themselves. That's how health care decisions are made. Health care decisions are personal and up to each individual. I'm kind of surprised you didn't know that being a doctor and all you asshole.

Dr. Fauci agreed with the President of our country when Joe Biden stated companies like Facebook and Twitter were killing people by allowing disinformation about the coronavirus vaccine to spread online. What many people don't seem to understand is the science on all of this was not a settled matter. Many doctors and scientists disagreed with the government, Dr. Fauci and big pharma, but they were silenced and shamed. That's not how a debate is supposed to be nor is it beneficial to any of us.. Facebook, Twitter, Reddit, and YouTube all were working hand in hand being good government agents. In October of 2020 YouTube amended its terms of service to include it would remove all content related to the Great Barrington Declaration and YouTube was extremely strict with all its content creators and if you dared speak out on any Covid related policy you were censored, suspended and your livelihood threatened. Free press, free country my ass. Fauci pretty much lied about everything and oftentimes Dr. Fauci lied in order to get the public to do what he wanted. For instance, in attempting to increase vaccination rates with dangling the carrot of herd immunity Dr. Fauci increased the number based on polls. So when polls indicated about 50% of the population would take the vaccine, Dr. Fauci said herd immunity would happen when about 70-75% of the country got vaccinated. As time went on and the propaganda was working and increasing Americans' confidence to get vaccinated, polls rose and now 60% of the American population said they would get vaccinated. Hearing this news in Dr. Fauci's own words "I thought I can nudge this up a bit, so I went to 80-85%" How can you trust anything this lying leprechaun says? You can't because he is speaking on behalf of his and others financial interests. I just watched a hilarious video on the Jimmy Dore Show on Dr. Fauci changing his statement on every issue there was, and sometimes he even contradicted himself in the same interview. Anyway I'm sure I'll come across more lies, but for now I've had enough and we will move on to another greedy, lying dirtbag.

Bill 'the pedophile and profiteer' Gates

I'm continuing to use my Donald Trump inspired nicknames. I have no idea why as a country Bill Gates was one of the main individuals we decided to put on a pedestal and give us medical direction on what we should all be doing during Covid. Is it simply because he's a billionaire who has the Mr. Rogers look going on? The very first thing I know about Bill Gates is, Bill isn't qualified to tell you or I shit about what we should do when it comes to our health care. I'll touch base on the first part of his nickname then we will get into what is more relevant to this Covid chapter topic. I don't know that we will ever find the proof that Bill Gates is a pedophile, but there certainly is plenty of common sense evidence that he did something devious. First let me say I don't think Bill Gates was having Jeffrey Epstien get him little girls to have sex with so I don't think he's the worst of what we conjure in our heads when we think of pedophiles. However, I'm not quite dumb enough to believe Mr. Gates' explanation as to why he contacted and met with Jeffrey Epstien. Gates gives a couple ridiculous, non believable reasons as to why he met with sex trafficker Jeffrey Epstein. The first explanation Bill gave to meet Epstein was somehow Gates believed Epstein would be the guy he should meet and speak with in order to help him win the Nobel Peace Prize. Really? You're Bill Gates, a famous billionaire who can get anyones ear and you choose to get the advice of a convicted sex offender?? Come on Bill, you obviously didn't think that lie through very well. Unless, somehow Bill thought some of the 16 year old girls Epstein knew might be the daughters of those who could help Bill get the Nobel Peace Prize. That's Bill, always thinking outside of the box, that's what makes him such a genius. In a May 22nd, 2021 businessinsider.com article titled "Bill Gates hoped his friendship with sex offender Jeffrey Epstein would help him win the Nobel Peace Prize, according to an ex-staffer who told the DailyBeast "He thought that Jeffrey would be able to help him, that he would know the right people or some kind of way massage things, so he could get the Nobel Peace Prize." I'm not sure, but was he trying to be funny using the word "massage"? If not, that may be the most ironic use of a word ever seeing that Epstein loved paying young females to give him massages.

Gates first met Epstein back in 2011 which was three years after the sicko Epstein had been convicted of soliciting sex from a minor. I hope anyone reading this understands there is zero chance billionaire, Bill Gates didn't have Jeffrey Epstein vetted before meeting with him therefore Mr. Gates was 100% aware of who he was meeting and what Epstein brought to the table was not financial advice or advice on winning the Nobel Peace Prize, no, it was young women that Epstein with the help of Ghislaine Maxwell brought to the table. I'm sure Melinda Gates knows much more than she is revealing considering she divorced the billionaire after 27 years of marriage and 34 years together as a couple. Gates met with Epstein numerous times at Epstein's Manhattan townhouse and by now everyone has read Bill's quote about Epstein stating "His lifestyle is very different and kind of intriguing although it would not work for me." What the fuck is so intriguing about a sex offender? Maybe Bill didn't have Epstein get him any young females. Maybe they sat in his townhouse discussing what Epstein does and looking at pictures of girls that are too young, but I am certain they did something they shouldn't have.

The second explanation Bill had for meeting with Epstein was he wanted to discuss philanthropic work with Epstein. Gates told the Wall Street Journal "There were people around him who were saying hey, if you want to raise money for global health and get more philanthropy, he knows a lot of rich people." Again, why on earth would Bill Gates have to go to a convicted sex offender to discuss charity work? It's simple, Mr. Gates wouldn't. Much of what went on during Covid, I knew was wrong and I knew using nothing more than common sense and common sense is all that is needed here. According to an October 12th, 2019 New York Times article by Emily Flitter and James B. Stewart, in March of 2013 Mr. Gates flew from New Jersey to Palm Beach, Florida on Mr. Epstein's Gulfstream plane even though Mr. Gates has his own private plane. In a March 2023 interview with ABC host Sarah Ferguson, Gates tried to seriously downplay his relationship with Epstein by repeating this answer in various ways "I will say for the hundredth time. I shouldn't have had dinners with him."

Gates was clearly frustrated with being asked questions about his relationship with Epstein and while attempting to downplay the relationship I believe Bill lost about 10 pounds from sweating as he was obviously extremely nervous. I won't spend any more time on this, but unless you are in denial, which people who are fans of Bill are, there is no way you can evaluate Bill Gates's relationship with Jeffrey Epstein and not conclude something nefarious was going on. I'm not 100% what was going on, but I know it was something shady.

Okay, so besides being a possible pedophile what else can we point out about Mr. Gates to see if he is or isn't qualified to lead you through your next health scare. Let's start with Bill's education; As far as education goes does Mr. Gates have a background in health care? No, Mr. Bill certainly does not. Mr. Gates did however get into Harvard Law School, where he later dropped out. This isn't a knock on Bill though. Gates is clearly intelligent and as far as proving it academically Gates scored a 1590 out of a 1600 total on his SATs so Bill is an extremely intelligent dude, but intelligence isn't the question. The question would be is Bill Gates qualified to make healthcare decisions for you? And of course the answer is a resounding no. Gates was apparently such an expert on Covid and its vaccines that Bill was able to advise the U.S. government on what countries the U.S. should be sending their Covid cash to. Through the Gates Foundation Bill also had great influence in other countries. In a letter to the German Chancellor Angela Merkel, Bill and Melinda Gates wrote "It is not too soon to start thinking about the next pandemic." A person and a group that had tremendous power and gained even more power and wealth during the pandemic says there will 100% be another pandemic. Well that's not scary. The narrative that another pandemic in our lifetimes is not inevitable. Maybe one on a much smaller scale, but it's not a foregone conclusion and if they feel that way the focus should be on prevention, not treatment with further lockdowns and more forced vaccinations. Gates pretended getting the vaccine out was an altruistic act, but it never was. Money and power have always been at the forefront during the Covid pandemic. Poor countries didn't have the same excess to the Covid vaccines due to an obvious lack of money, so an easy way around this would be for the pharmaceutical companies to share their intellectual properties with poorer countries. It's not as if the pharmaceutical companies actually paid for their own research and development in the first place. I'm assuming the generous Mr. Gates would be all for the sharing of this life saving intellectual property, but as it turns out Bill and the Gates Foundation were highly against the sharing of vaccine patents. I find it kind of humorous that Albert Bourla the Chief Executive of Pfizer when asked about sharing intellectual property stated "I have to say at this point in time, I think it's nonsense and at this point in time it's also dangerous." Yes, of course what Mr. Bourla was referring to was the fact that sharing Covid vaccine information would be dangerous to their enormous profits. What I meant by it being funny is that as it turned out old Albert Bourla was correct, sharing their vaccines is dangerous and looking back I'm sure the Continent of Africa which has done pretty well during Covid is probably thankful they didn't have a policy of forced vaccination. So on behalf of African countries thank you Mr. Bourla, you greedy prick.

Instead of sharing intellectual property, what the Gates foundation, pharmaceutical companies and other corporations and organizations that were profiting from the Covid cash cow wanted was for the vaccines to be donated. This way the vaccine would be sold to a more wealthy country like the U.S., Britain, France or Germany then donated to poorer countries. It's another way money is funneled to corporations through the guise of charity work. However real charitable groups like Doctors Without Borders vehemently disagreed with Gates's position.

Gates had tremendous political influence and set government agenda through the Gates Foundation and a couple other non-profits which Gates has close ties to including Gavi, the Vaccine Alliance, the Wellcome Trust, and CEPI, the Coalition for Epidemic Preparedness Innovations. According to Politico in a special report written by Erin Banco, Ashleigh Furlong and Lennart Pfahler titled 'How Bill Gates and partners used their clout to control the global Covid response - with little oversight', the four organizations gave 1.4 billion dollars to the WHO and that number has risen even higher as this article was written towards the end of 2022. People in the U.S. and around the world looked to organizations such as the WHO to provide crucial guidance during the pandemic, but it appears influence and conclusion prevented anyone from being unbiased. These organizations didn't stop with the WHO in spreading their money around. According to Politico the organization's leaders had unprecedented access to the highest levels of governments and spent almost 8.5 million dollars in lobbying. Don't worry, just as when all those other influential corporations spend millions in lobbying it comes back to them tenfold when the government then steals our money and gives it to those same organizations/corporations that were doing the lobbying. It's a fantastic, time proven system they have. Well, not so fantastic for us, but trust me none of these people gives a shit about us. To give an example from the Politico article CEPI spent $50,000 to get 200 million in yearly funding from the U.S. government and while that was waiting for congressional approval President Biden's budget allowed for 100 million dollars for five years going to CEPI. See it all works out for them. In the chapter 'Democrats and Republicans, A One Party System?' I write about how the relationship between Congress and the lobbyists is a revolving door with many of those leaving Congress getting jobs as lobbyists or "advisors" or the lobbyists getting jobs within the government. The exact same sort of conspiratorial arrangement has happened within this Covid lobbying arrangement. That's why everyone is so easily on the same page. All their interests aligned and even though their interests clashed with facts and science, it didn't matter because they all were supporting the same narrative so it made it appear that the facts had to be on their side. Bill Gates using his status and influence was constantly on our televisions giving interview after interview as if he were a scientist or the fascist leader of the U.S. or some other country. Mr. Gates was driven by profit and now Mr. Gates's tune has changed somewhat. Gates pushed and pushed the vaccine and the Bill and Milinda Gates foundation benefited tremendously. Now Gates has sold his stock and thus pivoted his position. Gates now says the vaccines are "not very effective" and "the virus isn't that dangerous except for the older population". Yet colleges still force the young to get vaccinated which is absolutely ridiculous. In part the government loves that they have completely brainwashed the younger generations. So, for me the worry is so much of the population is still unaware they were duped and they have no idea how easy the conspiracy comes together because they were willing participants. People picture a conspiracy as a group of people in a room making plans, possibly evil plans, but that's not how it works with most of the issues that keep the general population in the dark and obeying. What is going on is class solidarity. All these corporations and billionaires have the same interests so there is no need for them to meet. Just know Bill Gates and the rest of the billionaires, along with these corporations have interests that do not align with your interests. That being said, that will bring me to my next topic that follows up on this point.

Pandemic Profits

The money made during the pandemic is in the trillions of dollars. This was an enormous money grabbing opportunity for wealthy people and wealthy corporations. It's really impossible for someone like myself and probably you, the reader, to fathom that kind of money. Even when we are talking about billionaires it's hard to put it into context so we can get our heads around it, but we all dream about spending huge sums of money and buying whatever we want etc., so let's think of it this way; Let's pretend you had a billion dollars in your spare bedroom and you went in there and grabbed $5000.00 every day to spend, it would take you over 500 years to spend that money! At least you'll have the best medical care to make sure you live a long life. Time is a great way of looking into the massive difference between a millionaire and a billionaire. It takes a quick 11 days to get to a million seconds, but to reach a billion seconds it takes over 31 years! Put a couple other ways; if you made minimum wage it would take you over 65,000 years to earn a billion dollars (minimum wage varies in different states). Last example, if you saved $100.00 per day, 365 days a year, it would take you 27,397 years and 26 days to earn a billion dollars. Now as a country our government spent trillions so the math to put that into perspective is

1 million x 1,000 = 1 billion

1 billion x 1,000 = 1 trillion

So to put it into our terms, that's a lot of fucking money. There were all kinds of winners and losers during the pandemic, but in general it's fair to say the rich got richer the middle class got poorer and the poor, well they just stayed poor. More billionaires were made than ever during the pandemic. Large corporations profited while small businesses were crushed. In my opinion it was done on purpose. Businesses like Walmart and Target were allowed to stay open, but if you were a small business owner you were forced to close. Again this isn't a wacky conspiracy. Corporations and billionaires rule the world so their interests align and they basically crushed the little competition they had. Unfortunately, no retail type of business profited more than Amazon. Amazon's profits have boomed due to people being forced to stay in their homes or too scared to even go to their local corporate owned grocery store chain. At the start of the pandemic in March of 2020 Amazon did an extra 5 billion in sales in the first 3 months and in the first quarter of 2021 Amazon reported a profit of $8.1 billion, compared to 2.5 billion in the first quarter the year before.

Although Amazon profited because of governmental policies at least they didn't receive taxpayer money for their goods only to sell them back to us at a huge profit like some of the big pandemic winners in the pharmaceutical industry were able to do. The research was primarily funded by us, the taxpayers and then sold back to the same taxpayers at enormous profits. The cost to make a vaccine dose is approximately $1.80 and then the idiots in our government bought it back at a cost of about $20.00 per dose. Can you imagine in your life where this would ever be possible? I mean that's a great gig right there, if you can get it of course. Hopefully you aren't thinking "yeah but, the shots were free for us" You can't be. I mean I think a lot of Americans felt it was free, but I'm assuming if you are reading this book you understand nothing is free and we are paying for every dose, and for a vaccine that oh, by the way doesn't work very well.

According to Tim Bierley of Global Justice Now, Pfizer, Moderna and BioNTech have been making $1000.00 per second in profit on the coronavirus vaccines. Put together Pfizer, BioNTech, Moderna and Sinovac made an exorbitant $90 billion dollars in profits on their Covid-19 vaccines and medicines in 2021 and 2022. Pfizer was the biggest winner raking in $35 billion in net profits, while BioNTech and Moderna each pulled in $20 billion and poor Sinovac only stole $15 billion dollars from the taxpayer. It really shows us again how lobbying pays off for these corporations. A child would know that if they pay to create a product for someone and then have to buy that product back from them then you should get a great price so why doesn't the government know this. They do, but they just don't care. It's our money, not theirs. I think it would have been fairly easy to set limits on the profits that can be made. The companies are producing the product so there's nothing wrong with them being compensated and compensated well, but there could have easily been limits set so as to not punish the taxpayer during a global pandemic. If the pharmaceutical companies would have funded the research themselves then I guess they could have told us to fuck off, but they didn't and they pretty much never do. At a minimum the funding could have been considered a loan. The U.S. provided $5 billion dollars to seven vaccine producers to develop a vaccine so there was never any risk taken by the producer. To kick the taxpayer even more when they are down the government signed Advanced Purchase Agreements where the pharmaceutical companies were given money to research, develop and produce a vaccine and if the vaccine never came to fruition then the buyer lost out. There was no shared loss. What happened to these corporations and the U.S.'s love for capitalism because that sure sounds like some socialist shit there. According to the Peoples Vaccine Alliance the amount of money these companies received was approximately a whopping $90 billion dollars. In these Advanced Purchase Agreements Johnson and Johnson had a $1 billion dollar contract for 100 million doses. Moderna had an almost $5 billion dollar contract for 300 million doses, while Pfizer had a contract for almost $6 billion dollars for their 300 million doses.

I'm not sure if Pfizer, BioNTech and Moderna are using the bullshit excuse of inflation or if they see demand is falling for their faulty product that is potentially killing thousands of people, but the three companies have announced they will be upping the price of the vaccine to keep profits high. To make matters even worse if that's even possible the two U.S. based companies Pfizer and Moderna paid tax rates of only 15% and 7%

respectively. BioNTech is based in Germany and apparently the German government isn't quite as corrupt as the United States's with allowing corporations to get away with murder as BioNTech pays a tax rate of 31%. The politicians in the U.S. that all allow these and almost all corporations to pay these absurdly low tax rates should be ashamed of themselves. Of course the politicians are not ashamed of themselves. The politicians are actually quite proud because they know they get benefits in the form of campaign contributions or jobs or positions on boards.

Meanwhile, the United States citizens are stuck paying the highest rates for prescription drugs in the entire world with one out of four adults unable to afford their prescribed medications. Yet the top 50 executives in the top ten pharmaceutical companies took home approximately $2 billion dollars in compensation and stock awards. When the CEO of Moderna, Stephane Bancel resigns he will receive a $926 million dollar retirement package and the reality is Moderna makes all its money with the Covid vaccinations so we are paying his salary and his ridiculous exiting package. Forbes estimates that Mr. Bancels' worth is about $6 billion dollars. WTF Mr. Bancel you could at least send out some thank you cards to us citizens who have made you one of the newly created Covid billionaires. Moderna itself accounted for four of the new Covid billionaires. This honestly should infuriate the American public because this is the largest transfer of wealth from struggling taxpayers to corporations and corporate executives that has ever taken place. As I'm writing this I have to stop occasionally as I am overwhelmed with sadness and anger as I think about the Greedflation that we are currently stuck in and I wonder when and how is this ever going to end. This is what capitalism looks like in its current, most rotten form. It's socialism for many corporations like banks, oil companies and big pharma when it comes to risk, but pure capitalism when it's time for the profits. It's not just with the Covid vaccine where the taxpayer pays the expense for research and development. For example, according to healthaffairs.org between 2000 and 2019 well over $15 billion dollars was spent on HIV vaccine research with 80% of that money coming from the U.S. taxpayer. Furthermore, the Congressional Budget Office estimated that BARDA, the Biomedical Research and Development Authority, spent over 19 billion on Covid-19 vaccine development.

Also, in an article written by Richard G. Frank, Leslie Dach, and Nicole Lurie 'It Was The Government That Produced Covid-19 Vaccine Success' their research points out "Barda has for years invested in the messenger RNA (or mRNA) platform for vaccine development, the technology used in the Pfizer and Moderna COVID-19 vaccines. Since 2006, Congress has appropriated hundreds of millions of dollars that BARDA used to develop the scientific infrastructure to produce vaccines in response to the threat of pandemic flu." The authors point this out along with many other facts about how much money the government/public has invested in the Covid-19 vaccine, along with other vaccines as a fantastic thing and I guess I can agree with that assessment if the government didn't then give the information to the pharmaceutical companies for them to use it, produce the vaccine, and then sell it back to us at in insanely high price. How does anyone think this is okay? Let's pretend there are no pick up trucks in the world. So the government recognizes the need for said product and the government then takes hundreds of millions of dollars of your money and they make the plans and then they go to Ford and say "hey Mr. Ford, we designed the F-150 pick up truck, and we want you to produce it and then we will buy it back from you at 10x whatever it costs you to produce it". Mr. Ford says "wow, that's a pretty good deal for us. Would you like us to pay you for the plans, or at least pay back the money you used to invent the truck?" The government responds "No, of course not, the dumb ass taxpayer paid for it anyway so what we will do now is we will give them the trucks after we buy them from you and tell them it's free". Mr. Ford says "That won't work, they are going to know you are lying and lose their minds." The government just laughs and says "No, they won't mind at all. We will tell them they need the pick up truck. That if they don't take an F-150 pick up truck they will die and they will even kill their neighbors and get this, their grandmothers. Also, if they don't take the truck we won't let them go to work, thus if they want to feed their families they better take the damn truck." Mr. Ford says "wow, you're good, you kind of remind me of the Nazi's back in WWII. Is the truck safe?" The government replied "We don't know for sure, but we will find out and because we have plans to control all the media the American public won't find out for years so to come so no worries. We got you, just go make your billions and don't forget about us come election time my friend."

As I'm reading various articles and going to various government oversight pages etc. I"m seeing the money just doesn't end. Everywhere you turn there is a different aspect of the vaccine being funded that you may not have even thought about. When it came to the safety and if the vaccines would even work the federal government threw another $2.7 billion at Johnson and Johnson, Moderna, Sanofi, and AstraZeneca to cover those expenses. God forbid these fucking companies come out of their pockets for anything. You wouldn't want to keep going out for dinner and drinks with these people as your only friends. Also Covid profits weren't just limited to vaccine sales. Think about all the money made by mask manufacturers, Covid testing etc. The pandemic was a boom for lobbyists because once an industry gets the government purchasing their products they do not want that money to stop so they form a lobby and then buy our politicians. That's the American way, 100%.

Consequences from Lockdowns and Scare Tactics

There were so many harmful consequences from the government's lockdown policies and scare tactics that we will unfortunately be seeing the negative effects for years to come. Mental health went untreated and skyrocketed due to a complete lack of social interaction during the pandemic. Individuals stopped going to their physicians to be treated for conditions or to be tested for possible health concerns in which we usually screen for. For example, the CDC's National Breast and Cervical Cancer Early Detection Program reports that the total number of cancer screenings decreased by an average of 87% for breast cancer and 84% for cervical cancer at the start of the pandemic. Among poorer people screening declined at an even higher rate. The CDC estimates that among Native American women and Alaskan Native women breast cancer screenings declined an astonishing 98%. All cause deaths are up 32% for the general population and lack of medical care during the pandemic has certainly contributed to that steep increase. Among younger individuals the all cause death increase is up 40%! Young athletes have been dropping dead at an alarming rate yet the mainstream media which has generated millions in advertising from big pharma won't dare to cover such a topic because we all know there is really only one main thing that has changed in the last few years to cause such an increase among young people. Cough, cough, (the vaccine) cough, cough (the vaccine). I understand the difference between there being a correlation and causation, but once there is a strong correlation you have to investigate to show if there is a causation or not. Unfortunately that won't happen in the U.S. and if it does happen it will be run by those who do not wish for the truth to come out.

The CDC has confirmed approximately 130,000 children and young adults have "died suddenly" in the U.S. since the Covid-19 vaccines have been given. So this would be for 2021 and 2022 and not 2020 when the most dangerous of the Covid strains was causing havoc among the old, sick and obese. I see article after article defending the vaccine and stating that the increase is due to other issues and not the vaccine. One propagandas article on apnews.com by Karena Phan and Ali Swenson attributes the excess deaths to the delta variant, but there is simply no data or science to back that claim up. The delta variant was a weaker, more spreadable variant and young people were not dying from the Covid delta variant. As a matter of fact people aged up to 30 years and under only accounted for 8,268 covid related deaths from 2019 to February 1st, 2023 and we already know those numbers early on were inflated because no matter what you died from early on if you had Covid they automatically listed your cause of death as being from Covid. Young people have also had a large increase in suicides, but apparently most people feel "fuck the young". I recently had a conversation with a friend who was telling me about how her son was a highly successful athlete and he lost all those important sports years as he was going into his first year of college. He became so depressed that he attempted to kill himself. Suicide rates soared during the pandemic among the ages of 5-24 and according to the CDC there was also a huge increase in suicide attempts. In the winter of 2021 suicide attempts rose nearly 40%! But go ahead and pretend you care about people while locking kids down and forcing them to wear masks all while you knew they were never at real risk of dying from Covid. I went to my step son, Aaron Shareef's graduation at the end of June, 2023 and listened to the valedictorian's speech and it was so sad. The young girl talked about all they went through dating back to the 9th grade when Covid started, masking, lockdowns, mental health problems, isolation, lack of any activities, etc. etc. I was both sad for those students and all the students around the country and angry at the government who unnecessarily put all these kids through hell for no reason whatsoever.

When I first moved to Los Angeles people were very friendly, smiling and interacting with other strangers as LA is a city filled with individuals who are transplants from other cities and states who often don't know anyone. Once the pandemic hit, everything changed. Do to fear, everyone wore a mask and if you were outside without a mask people would literally run away from you. I'm not joking or exaggerating. Even though I was respectful and followed the social distancing recommendations people would literally run away from me as if getting anywhere near my maskless self would instantly kill them. Many people like myself were in complete isolation. I'm pretty much a loner so for me the isolation was no big deal, but for many the isolation of Covid was horrific. For senior citizens who had a legitimate health concern from Covid the isolation was not one easily dealt with because they truly had to balance seeing friends or family with the concern of catching a virus that could possibly end their lives.

Young people, however, were isolated for no good reason. Younger individuals have healthy, robust immune systems and many people acquired natural immunity, but both were ignored by the government and mainstream media and it was portrayed as if Covid-19 was equally deadly to a young healthy person as it was for a senior citizen with multiple health problems. In Los Angeles we are in the summer of 2023 presently and it's young people I see outside by themselves wearing masks more than anyone else. Many young people have been completely brainwashed by our government and never has one of my favorite sayings by the famous Irish author 'George Bernard Shaw' been more true; "youth is wasted on the young."

Lockdowns were not effective because we needed healthy people to live their lives and if they caught Covid as I did three times they would be fine just as I was. Don't get me wrong. I didn't try to catch Covid just as I don't try to catch the flu. If someone is sick I stay away from them and if I am sick I stay home away from others. The first time I caught Covid was horrible. I was very sick and my cough and general weakness lingered for months. The second time I had Covid was like a minor cold and the third time I had Covid was kind of a level of sickness that was in between the first and second times. I lived though and even though the first time was fairly horrible I have had the flu worse. Viruses are no joke and you can see how they could kill you, but the negative effects on mental health, the economy, education and the social structure have outweighed any risks from Covid. Plus most of all, to spite all the lockdowns, masking requirements and vaccine mandates almost everyone still caught Covid!

Children and young people in high school also paid an extremely high price during the Covid lockdowns. Young children showed changes in their emotional growth and if that child had a learning disability then the consequences were even greater. Children often developed sleep disorders due to some changes in their routine. There was also an emotional cost to many children seeing their parents struggle during lockdowns. In poor areas many kids and parents relied on schools to make sure their kids had breakfast and lunch. Kids today already struggle compared to past generations with getting enough physical activity in their lives and this was only exacerbated during lockdowns where kids were kept away from their peers and gym class no longer existed. Many children and teens were now introduced to feelings such as depression and anxiety for the first time in their lives. Kids were also worried they would catch Covid and possibly die or get their family members sick. Young children and teenagers missed seeing friends, family and playing sports. High school kids missed their senior years in football, basketball, wrestling, swimming etc and there is no going back and reliving their last year. Proms and school dances etc. were all canceled. Students were robbed of what many kids enjoy about being in school and all just to control, brainwash and force a vaccine on them.! In my opinion making kids and teenagers wear masks was a big part of the government's agenda. The government wanted to teach these generations that they need to unquestionably listen to their government and that their government was there to protect them and guide them and they should listen and do exactly as they are told. The brainwashing of society on the whole has worked pretty well during Covid, but wow, that brainwashing has worked perfectly on the young. Again, "youth is wasted on the young." I'm honestly not sure if the damage done during Covid lockdowns can ever be overcome and in part it's because the government saw how easily most Americans were manipulated and complied without question to everything.

Women also seemed to fare poorly under Covid lockdowns and during Covid restrictions in general. For various reasons worldwide women suffered from increased violence at home. The reasons stem from being as simple as both partners were highly stressed and also were around each other much more if they lost their job or were perhaps working from home. As someone who has never hit a woman it's hard to fathom that being around your partner more enabled you to abuse them physically. I understand mentally it must have been difficult and I'm sure some couples fought more than they ever have in the past, but I would think if you don't hit women, you don't hit women and if you do, you do so maybe the violence just showed up more. The negative effects on women extended to their mental health as women suffered mental health issues at a much higher rate than men did. According to a journal article in Economic Policy titled 'The impact of the coronavirus lockdown on mental health: evidence from the United States' "As a result of the lockdown measures, the existing gender gap in mental health has increased by 61%."

In states that did not impose lockdowns or lifted them after only a few days mental health issues were far less frequent compared to states like NY and California that were like Nazi regimes during the pandemic imposing lockdowns every time Covid infection numbers rose. To me that was one of the most ridiculous aspects of the lockdowns; Covid numbers would fall and we were allowed to eat outside, but parks and many other activities were still closed or restricted. Then Covid infection would increase and bam, lockdowns again, everything is shut down, stay in your homes etc. The issue was we were never going to get to zero so how long were we going to play this stupid game? It could have gone on forever and as it was the lockdown restrictions went on far too long especially here in California.

The government and news organizations teamed up to use scare tactics in commercials and news reports to instill fear into people that still has not gone away. Phrases like "Stay home to save lives" or "If you go outside you can either get it or spread it, and people will die" Almost never were facts on who was most at risk drilled home. Older individuals, obese individuals, people with comorbidities, often caused by obesity were the groups who were at a much higher risk. There should have been a national call to each individual to take control of their own health; to use this time to start an exercise program and start eating healthy. Instead of closing gyms, maybe the government should have closed fast food restaurants like McDonalds, Burger King, Wendy's, Kentucky Fried Chicken and Taco Bell. God forbid we speak about the fact that being obese is a serious health concern. Instead the government chose to keep you out of parks where you could get fresh air (sort of fresh) , go for walks, and see people. No, stay in your homes or you will surely die and kill your grandmother in the process.

News organizations constantly showed images of people

dying with respirators on and being kept away from their loved ones. There never was a separation of those who died because of Covid and those who died 'with Covid'. I read an article recently about a poor 14 year old boy who had brain cancer. The young boy suffered immensely, going through every treatment possible including chemo, radiation and surgeries. The tumor grew so large that it came out of the protrude outward on the top of his head. Hospice was finally brought in after every option had been tried and failed. Eventually the young boy had to be brought to the hospital to help better deal with his pain levels and end of life care. After he passed away a government official listed him as the first person under 15 years of age to die of Covid because he ended up contracting Covid while in the hospital. This was simply another scare tactic as in this case Covid was not even listed as a cause of death on the young man's death certificate. This is all part of the scare tactics used to keep people in their homes, to keep schools closed and ensure high vaccination rates.

Honesty was never even considered because honesty is not something the government is familiar with. According to dailymail.co.uk a government memo shared in March 2020 suggested "The perceived level of personal threat needs to be increased among those who are complacent" They wanted everyone in masks and to feel getting Covid was a death sentence and yes, the first strain of Covid was dangerous, but just going by the numbers it was far from a death sentence and if you were not in a risk category then you should be every bit as careful as you are when you try to avoid getting the flu. Now as we are going in the late part of 2023 Covid is equivalent to the common cold for most people yet they are still pushing the vaccine! The vaccine is not being pushed nearly as bad as it was before, but it's still being pushed and colleges are still requiring it! That's insane! College kids are at almost zero risk from Covid, but do you know why colleges are still requiring students to be vaccinated? If you are following the theme here I bet you can guess it has something to do with money. Yep, pharmaceutical companies have been donating big money to universities in order for those universities to keep their ridiculous vaccination policies. The pharmaceutical industry along with the government and businesses has used all sorts of punishments in order to attempt to force everyone to get vaccinated. President Biden signed an executive order requiring federal contractors and subcontractors to get vaccinated. The Centers for Medicare and Medicaid Services (CMS) required some 17 million employees of Medicare and Medicaid participating hospitals and health care facilities to be vaccinated. Biden required all federal employees to be vaccinated or lose their job. Also, the Occupational Safety and Health Administration had sent to the White House a bullshit emergency regulation that mandated all employers with more than 100 workers to require vaccinations or weekly COVID tests. Private industry jumped on board and went along with vaccination requirements trying to force people to either get the shot or lose their job, again, making it a choice between feeding your family or putting some foreign substance in your body that you don't want, nor need. If you were unvaccinated, Delta Airlines charged employees an extra $200.00 per month for their health insurance premium. The government and industry used every immoral means to try to force everyone to get vaccinated and unfortunately they are not through with some of us yet.

Final Thoughts

What we lived through was one of the worst and most shameful periods in American history. Oh, and not just the U.S., all around the globe various countries who preach freedom and democracy became authoritarian States. Canada and Australia were both shameful. When the Canadian truckers protested, Canada's scumbag Prime Minister Justin Trudeau invoked Canada's 'Emergencies Act' and shut down crowdfunding and froze bank accounts of anyone who even donated to help the demonstrators. That was not very Canadian of you Mr. T. Again, countries using the strategy of if you want to eat, thus live, you are going to do as we say and take that vaccine that does nothing and potentially will harm you. Australia, not to be outdone, had their police force attack anyone who did not adhere to their lockdowns. From Australia's police point of view, old ladies sitting on a park bench were dangerous criminals and were treated as such. The worst part is it will happen again and more then likely the government will pull the same bullshit as they did this time. Why? Because too many Americans remain ignorant. The other day I went to an Art festival with a cousin of mine who in the summer of 2023 still thinks Covid is dangerous. I was blown away. He's someone who doesn't trust our government. He understands the government continuously lies to us and he also knows the greed of corporations like those in the pharmaceutical industry, yet he still believes every lie both the government and big pharma have told us. I ran into an old friend at the festival who was wearing a mask. I don't understand how someone is still wearing a mask outside in the summer of 2023. Then when I commented to my cousin that at this point for most people Covid is equivalent to the common cold and it is not dangerous he vehemently disagreed with me. Covid being equivalent to the common cold for most people at this point is not my opinion, it's a fact supported by the data. All you follow the science, people have actually never once followed the science. No, you only listened to what you were told by your side. You were told what to do and what to think and you went along unquestioning. The majority of Americans went along with masking, lockdowns, not seeing their friends and family, and getting vaccinated and were thankful to the government for it and that did not go unnoticed by our government. They were laughing and how easily most people were fooled and went along with everything they were told to do even while those who told you what to do did as they pleased. From Gavin Newsome having his family get togethers as if nothing was happening and while forcing us to wear masks, stay home and limiting family gatherings for fear of arrest to Boris Johnson and his conservative staff dancing and partying it up while you most of us dummies were forced to listen to these lying dirtbags and sit home by ourselves. I could scream, aaaah!!!!!!!!!!! There, I feel so much better. I'm still so angry though. There won't be a reckoning. No one who caused this, who championed it, who bullied others and who profited will ever pay a price for what occurred during this Covid nightmare.

From the ESPN bullies like Micheal Wilbon, to those who controlled the narrative and what we were able to do like Bill Gates and Dr. Fauci, The only thing I can possibly hope for is for the truth to keep emerging. For people like myself, Jimmy Dore, Russel Brand, and Dr. John Campbell to keep pushing forward with the truth and hopefully eventually enough people will see they were lied to that the next time this happens they will stand up and refuse to be bullied in submission. That's our only hope, forget about real accountability, but we can have accountability in public opinion if enough people choose not to remain ignorant. We also have to force investigations into deaths that common sense points to the vaccine as the cause. Sudden cardiac arrest is the leading cause of death in young athletes and heart attacks from people under 60 are at an all time high. There has been a 30% increase in heart attacks in adults aged 25 to 44 and a 20% increase in adults 45 to 64. The Florida Department of Health found an 84% increase in the relative incidence of cardiac-related death among males aged 18 to 39 years old within 28 days following mRNA vaccination. High school athletes have been collapsing and sometimes dying all over the country. We know in the U.S. all these athletes were forced to be vaccinated so again using common sense the vaccine could be the cause. The biggest indication as there was not an increase in 2020 when Covid-19's was most dangerous. You have to understand no one in the mainstream will say the vaccine is the cause. The news organizations are funded by the pharmaceutical companies through advertising. I'm listening to a video by Dr. John Campbell at the moment and it's hilarious that everyone is so scared of the censorship that he gives a disclaimer before he goes over that data that he is not saying "the vaccines aren't safe and effective" Jimmy Dore half jokingly does that every time he goes over data as well. Myself nor anyone else can't say for sure that the vaccine is causing the increase in deaths, but certainly the data is showing a correlation. As a matter of fact, looking worldwide there is a positive correlation between excess deaths and higher vaccination rates. So countries with the highest vaccination rates have the highest increase in mortality. Then there are deaths where I just don't need to see the data. I see teenagers dying of cardiac arrest all the time. I know that's not normal so what has changed to possibly cause these deaths? It's only one thing! Vaccinations. As I'm trying to find information it's disgusting because every article is just another attempt to refute that data and say "yes, but there is no evidence that the deaths are caused by the vaccines". We don't have a free press in the United States no matter what you may think. And yeah, there's no evidence because you aren't looking for it! Even when an article acknowledges the connection or heart problems associated with the vaccine they point out that they are "rare" and statistically they are correct but since there isn't really a valid reason for a healthy teenager to get the Covid-19 vaccine, rare is still too often. Also if that were your child I don't think you would care how rare the problems occur. Go read some of these heartbreaking stories and use your common sense and picture the teen in the story being your son or daughter. Also, young athletes were not dropping dead at this rate prior to vaccinations so you do the

Chapter 2-

Trump, Hillary/Biden, and Bernie

I've been a Bernie fan for many years so when I first heard Mr. Sanders was running for President I was very excited. I told anyone, and everyone who would listen, everything I knew about Bernie. In the early stages that's all I ever heard was that Bernie had no chance of beating Hillary. I suppose early on I had my doubts as well, but I also had this belief Bernie had to win. When he ran again against Joe Biden I thought or hoped he learned a few lessons and this time he was going to win. There's no one else in politics with Bernie's integrity and history of doing the right thing simply because it's the right thing. I'm grateful that we live in an era where information is everywhere, and can be seen in real time. I would see videos of Bernie rallies with thousands of energized people. You wouldn't have known that if you watched the news because they were dead set on only supporting the corporate owned mainstream Democrat to run for, and win the Presidency. I'm positive if this had been 10 or 15 years ago we would have never been aware of the grassroots movement that had taken place because the national media mostly ignored Bernie, and we would have not known any better. Eventually, Bernie would have had to get out of the race because people like myself would have given up. We would have thought we were the only ones who knew about Bernie, unaware there were thousands who were dying for the hope and change that Barack Obama only promised, but failed to deliver.

In both primaries the DNC, and the media did everything they could to help Hillary and Biden win. Donna Brazile, who was the interim chair of the Democratic National Committee when Hillary ran, leaked debate questions and topics to Hillary. These leaked debate questions should have been a huge story for the rest of the primary race, but it was almost dead immediately. Brazile thought she was doing her duty as the DNC chair, and she would do it again if that's what was necessary. During a radio interview with SiriusXM host Joe Madison, Brazile stated "if I had to do it all over again, I would know a hell of a lot more about Cybersecurity." CNN had no choice but to fire Brazile, but her punishment for betraying the voters, and democracy itself fell far short of what it should have been. I don't understand why this was brushed aside like it wasn't that big of a deal. Brazile admitted in an interview with the Washington Post that although she should be neutral she was not, and indeed she was "ready for Hillary." What bothered me even more about this scandal was Hillary Clinton was completely let off the hook for this. They remained silent in the days after the scandal hit the news, and the media helped by not being or remaining outraged. Hilary was hardly questioned as if she had no hand in this wrong doing. I don't think Bernie did himself any favors either by being the class act he is. Bernie failed to take advantage of this issue or any other issue as Bernie always refused to truly go after Hillary. I think in both primaries Bernie was worried that if he lost and damaged the Democratic candidate too much it would help Trump win. The difference the second time for me is I hold it against Bernie for not doing what needed to be done for us. Bernie knew what was being done, and he chose the Democratic Party over us again. I think in both primaries the worry of damaging Hillary or Biden was the prevailing thought for many nationally known individuals who "supported" Bernie.

Bill Maher is someone I admire, and respect so much, and who could have easily helped Bernie much more than he did. I think Mr. Maher is the best example I can think of in how he felt, and behaved while semi supporting Bernie. Mr. Maher refused to ever criticize Hillary for fear he would damage her, and thus help Trump. If he would have gone all in for Bernie, I believe Mr.

Maher would have helped keep the media a little more honest. Mr. Maher should have been all in for Bernie, and he wasn't. Even after the primaries, every time someone spoke up and disagreed with something that happened with Bernie, Mr. Maher would cut the person speaking right off. Being a huge Bill Maher fan, I watch Bill on HBO week in, and week out. Often, if not always, when someone speaks poorly, and truthfully about Hillary or anyone in the Democratic Party, Mr. Maher talks over them, and refuses to let them speak. I see that often on his show with him or if he has someone on his show like Barney Frank. Mr. Frank will speak over more liberal voices, and turn into a bully right before our very eyes. Mr. Frank did this on Maher's August 3rd show regarding Whistleblowers. Even Maher jokingly stated "You're badgering the witness Barney." Frank gives paid speeches to Wall Street now, and claims it's because "He's interesting" and of course defended Hillary for her paid speeches. Where does Mr. Barney Frank work now? Barney was elected on the board of directors for Signature Bank. Frank is another hypocrite that takes advantage of the influence he will have because of his former job. In an interview with the "Observer" Frank stated "The notion that banks are too influential--I think this is a mistake on part of some of my friends on the left, and maybe in general. The big banks do not have the political influence that people think they do." Okay Barney, how do you even say that bullshit without laughing your ass off? I recently watched a video where another person I truly admire, Cornel West, was criticizing Obama, and Al Sharpton was yelling over him so he could drown out the truth. I don't understand why you can't tell the truth about what someone is doing just because they are perceived to be on the same team as you.

Once the DNC, and the media got the Hillary and Biden victories they wanted, they thought all of us Bernie supporters should just jump on board the Hillary and Bidne trains. I can't tell you how angry this made almost all of us Bernie supporters. Although with Biden I think between many of us being so disappointed in Bernie and sick of Trump the Bernie supporters voted for Joe much more easily. I will never forget the time Sarah Silverman said to the Bernie or Bust people "You're being ridiculous" then she went on the Bill Maher show, and Mr. Maher tells Sara Silverman he "thought it was wonderful". It blows my mind how Bill, and Sarah just do not get it. Let me see if I can explain this to you Bill; We live in a semi free country, and we all get to make many choices. I was a high school teacher for a little while, and when I would give a test some kids would complain, and say they didn't want to take it. I would tell them, "You don't have to take the test, as a matter of fact you don't even have to stay here in class if you chose not to." I would tell the students "You are free to get up right now and leave. Of course the act of leaving may come with a consequence." So Hillary, and the DNC stole the primary election from Bernie, then you want us to pretend it didn't happen. Not only do you want us to pretend it didn't happen, but you want us to reward them for their behavior! No way, not a chance in hell were we going to do that!

If we did, the Democrats would do the same thing that they have always done. I guess my naivety showed up here because the lesson the DNC and the media learned after Hillary was not the lesson I hoped. Instead of being more fair when Bernie ran against Joe Biden the DNC and the media just took their cheating to new levels. Now for us, when it came to Hillary running against Donald Trump we understood that there would also be a consequence for us refusing to vote for Hillary, but we were willing to accept that. No way were we voting for Hillary, consequences be damned. We ended up with the horrible, horrible consequence of Donald Trump being elected our President. Even though we had to suffer the consequences, it was not our fault, it was yours! It was the DNC's! It was Hillary's!

Killer Mike was on Bill Maher after the election, and he explained nicely why he couldn't switch over to Hillary. Killer Mike stated "I saw a guy get robbed, and for all that was moral, and good about me I couldn't un-see that." Then, of course what Bill did was, he got mad, and really didn't let Killer Mike finish everything he wanted to say. Mike talked about how active Bernie has been, and how Bernie had "been in the streets" and how Hillary hadn't "been in the streets" and Bill cut him off. Fran Lebowitz was another Bill Maher guest who spoke disrespectfully about Bernie calling him a narcissist. What!? Bernie is about "we" not "I" and that is why we were all Bernie or Bust. So guess what Fran, you're the narcissist, so fuck you, fuck Hillary, and most of all, fuck the DNC.

I participated in politics for the first time because of Bernie. I have always loved politics, I love debating, and having discussions, but I never actually participated. This was the first time I donated, and donated multiple times. This is the first time I went to political rallies, and also met with other Bernie supporters. Bernie inspired myself and millions of others.

Let's take a look at Hillary's record: In 2002 Hillary, along with Joe Biden were two of the 77 senators who gave President George W. Bush the authority to use force in Iraq. I'm quite sure the reader already knows where Bernie stood on this issue. Like always, Bernie is on the right side of history before most others in our government are. Bernie leads, Hillary follows, and usually what Hillary follows is the money. Hillary spoke multiple times to Goldman Sachs, Morgan Stanley, Deutsche Bank, Kohlberg Kravis Roberts, and UBS Wealth Management for a whopping $225,000 each speech. Mrs. Clinton didn't just sell out to Wall Street, she also betrayed us by taking huge sums of money for her speeches to the Pharmaceutical industry. The National Association of Chain and Drug Stores, and the Healthcare Information and Management Systems Society both paid the hefty $225,000 dollar fee as well. I think we all understand that unless it's a roast, no one pays someone to say things they do not want to hear. What did she say? Who knows, and she will never release the speeches so until someone steals them we won't ever know what Hillary told her Wall Street friends.

Both Hillary and Joe were on the side of President Bush on homeland security as well, and in 2001 voted for the Patriot Act. Want to guess who didn't? I bet you guessed it, yep, Mr. Bernie Sanders. In case you thought she got caught up after 9/11 like she did with voting for the Iraq war, and once time passed Hillary was able to access the situation and rethink her position; you'd be wrong. When votes to renew the legislation in 2005 and 2006 came up, Hillary again voted in favor, while Bernie voted against. None of this is anything new, but it's the stuff Hillary supporters don't want to hear about or speak about. I'm glad Killer Mike, and Cornel West are two African Americans who didn't support Hillary because most African American communities have been fooled by the Democrats, and by the Clintons as well. Under Bill Clinton, funding for public housing decreased by $17 billion. Funding for corrections (which would cause African American families to be torn apart again) increased by 19 billion. For some reason our government seems to always find different ways to separate African Americans from the rest of us. I will cover this much more in my chapter about prisons, and also race.

I love Bill Maher. I even went to see him in early 2018 when Bill performed at Shea's in Buffalo, NY. I think from time to time Bill gets back to being the old Bill again except for those times where he shows me he still just doesn't get it when it comes to the Bernie supporters, and how we would never support Hillary or Joe for that matter, no matter what the consequence. Lastly, I see Hillary pop back up occasionally, and it's the last thing this country needs. I think she would love to run for President again, and is putting herself out there to see what people think.

Soooooo, please, crawl under a rock, and go away for about 70 or 80 years. Thanks!

So then we had to deal with the consequence, which was the nightmare Presidency of Donald Trump. We were reminded daily because with each new day, came a new scandal, a new embarrassing tweet, or some other controversy involving Trump or one of his moronic supporters. It's almost impossible to keep up with the news and scandals coming out of the Trump White House. As I was trying to write this book, the news was moving at lighting speed every day. I would have to keep telling myself "I'm not a newspaper. I can't keep addressing every scandal that comes out of the White House or I will never finish." The speed at which the news is moving makes me believe, or hope President Trump will be impeached by the time this book gets published. However, life goes on, and so I will plot forward, and hope for the best just as I did when Mr. Trump was running for President.

During the race for the Presidency I was honestly hopeful that if Trump won he wouldn't actually do anything he was saying, and that the mentally challenged Trump supporters would be very disappointed. I should have known better because Trump made his entrance into the current political landscape by continually claiming or wondering aloud if Obama had really been born in the United States. Perhaps it was with this attack on then President Obama where Mr. Trump first discovered his base. However, to spite this ridiculous claim there were still many reasons for me to hold on to my hope. On Meet the Press in 1999 while speaking to Tim Russert, Mr. Trump stated it wouldn't bother him at all if homosexuals serve openly in the military. Mr. Trump went on, and spoke about how he "is strongly for choice" concerning the subject of abortion. When it comes to the abortion issue I think Trump feels like many liberal minded people; We don't like abortions, but we are pro-choice. Unfortunately, Trump is stacked the Supreme Court with Justices who overturned

Roe v. Wade. The Supreme Court overturned the 1973 landmark decision affirming the constitutional right to abortion. The 6-3 ruling ended nearly 50 years of abortion rights. We all knew what was happening with Brett Kavanaugh, who is currently home drinking beers. We hoped President Trump would have to nominate another asshole for the Supreme Court, but a slightly less rapey, less drunk asshole then Kavanaugh. Unfortunately Mr. Kavanaugh was confirmed to the Supreme Court. The Supreme Court now has 6 conservative justices and because of the insane lifetime appointments that will probably not change anytime soon. What people who want to overturn Roe v. Wade fail to realize is making abortions illegal won't stop abortions from taking place. Unfortunately, abortions will move from the safety of a medical facility, performed by a doctor, to someone's house performed by Donald Trump with a hanger. Who knows, these backwards assholes may try to overturn the Thirteenth Amendment. I think the only amendment that is truly safe is the infamous Second Amendment.

Trump himself often had high opinions of the Democrats. In a 2004 interview with CNN's Wolf Blitzer, Mr. Trump stated "It just seems the economy does better under Democrats than the Republicans." In another interview with the same Wolf Blitzer this time in 2007, Trump actually praised Hillary Clinton. Mr. Trump felt Hillary would do a great job, be a tough negotiator, and could successfully work out a deal with Iran. Trump went on to state "Hillary's always surrounded herself with very good people. I think Hillary would do a good job." When it came to guns Mr. Trump's views for the most part were that of the mainstream. In Trump's book, "The America We Deserve", Trump wrote "I generally oppose gun control, but I support the ban on assault weapons, and I also support a slightly longer waiting period to purchase a gun." Those Trump views are views most Americans can live with, and most Americans agree with those opinions as well. Health care is another issue Donald covered, and believe it or not Mr. Trump was also on the liberal side in “The America We Deserve”. Covering the health care issue, Mr. Trump writes "We should not hear so many stories of families ruined by health care expenses. We must not allow citizens with medical problems to go untreated because of financial problems or red tape." Trump goes on to write "The Canadian plan also helps Canadians live longer, and healthier than America. We need, as a nation, to re-examine the single-payer plan, as many individual states are doing."

So what happened to this level-headed Donald Trump? I think as the Republican primaries got rolling he found what worked, and he went with it. At first I don't think Trump believed anything he was saying. I think if he lost he would have come clean, and said he only said those things because he knew he was appealing to all those hillbilly, crazy Republicans. Trump would have confessed he really believes they are a bunch of fools. I have a brother who is unfortunately a huge Trump fan, and I used to tell him all the time, "Trump doesn't believe anything he's saying. Trump is just saying those things because he knows it gets people like you all fired up, and if he loses he's going to admit he didn't believe anything he said.” The problem with Donald Trump is he's been playing the role now for so long he has now become the character he was only playing at the start. I think now Trump actually believes in the bullshit he spews because he played the part so well, for so long, he’s morphed into that over the top, crazy Donald Trump. I've heard of this type of thing happening to method actors. They get so intensely into a role that they have a hard time de-characterizing. Trump has become the character he was playing, and unfortunately for most of us the character he is playing is a crazy monster. That’s not to say, Trump was some amazing, kind person prior to the election, but I honestly do not believe he was ever as horrible as he is now.

One aspect of his Presidency that is a part of his true character because he's a spoiled rich kid is his undoing of anything good President Obama achieved. It's become his most important personal mission. We all know it started at the 2011 White House correspondent's dinner where President Obama roasted Mr. Trump for about five straight minutes. Obama being a fantastic orator was a natural, and because this was after Trump's birther bullshit, Obama truly enjoyed crushing Trump. Mr. Trump would never admit this but, believe me, the "N" word was being thrown around all night at the Trump residence that evening. The comical speech was so good some of it needs to be revisited here. "No one is happier, no one is prouder to put this birth certificate matter to rest than the Donald. That's because he can finally get back to focusing on the issues that matter, like: Did we fake the moon landing? What really happened in Roswell? And where are Biggie and Tupac?" The lines received huge laughs, and Donald was seething on the inside. Trust me, "N" word all night! President Trump is a 70 something year old child. President Trump is a complete embarrassment. I don't blame many people who wanted Trump to win the election. Hillary was a horrible candidate. Bernie should have been the Democratic nominee. I didn't want someone who has never met a war she didn't love to win. Hillary inspired those who hate her much more than those who liked her. Many reluctantly supported her, but it stemmed from the dislike of Trump rather than wanting Hillary as their President.

The issue I have with someone who was a Trump supporter is that if you supported him prior to the election, and now after seeing his behavior, after reading his tweets, after witnessing his policies, and then you still support him; To me, that says something about you as a person. I'm not talking about every single Trump supporter because I think some are just fooled and believe him when he says he's not part of the system, and even if he isn't, trust me he benefits from it and doesn't want any change. I still have my Bernie for President bumper sticker on my back windshield. Sometimes someone will ask me; why is it that I still have the Bernie sticker on my car? I explain it's because the Bernie bumper sticker says something about who I am as a person. It's not about Bernie. It's about inclusion, tolerance, and love. It says, I'm not a racist. It says, I care about others. Most importantly, it says, I'm not a dick. (Even though, truth be told, sometimes I am ☺). A Trump bumper sticker says the complete opposite, and those who drive with a Trump bumper sticker on are either too stupid to know that's what it means, or they are too much of an asshole to care.

Trump's cult members also do not care about facts. He can tweet something or be recorded on film making a statement, then the next day Mr. Trump can say it never happened, "it's fake news", and his supporters believe him. I've never seen anything like it. Mr. Trump correctly understood the stupidity of his supporters when at a rally in Sioux Center, Iowa, Trump stated "I could stand in the middle of Fifth Avenue and shoot somebody, okay, and I wouldn't lose any voters, okay? It's like, incredible". Trump was basically calling his stupid followers "stupid" and right to their face, but they were actually too stupid to realize it. Let's take a look at a few of Trump's policies starting with the tax cuts. The Trump tax cuts changed the corporate tax rate from 35% to 21%. The top rate of those earning $500,000 and up drops from 39.6% to 37%. The corporate tax cuts have no end date, while the individual tax cuts are set to expire in 2026. First off, that corporate rate of 35% is bullshit. Apple reports paying a tax rate of 25.8%, Microsoft 16.5%, Alphabet, which is the parent company of Google paid 19%. Twenty six Fortune 500 firms paid no federal income taxes at all from 2008 to 2012 including General Electric. General Electric seems to always find a way to continue to not only pay no taxes, but to receive a tax benefit. Last year General Electric earned a nice 10 billion while receiving 400 million dollar tax benefit, thus achieving a tax rate of -4.5%!!! That should infuriate Trumpers, but instead they are mad at the person working 30 hours a week at the Walmart collecting food stamps.

There is a common misconception that corporations flip the bill for most of the federal taxes collected. That's just simply not true. Individuals like you, and I contribute the largest portion of tax revenue. Income taxes contribute just below $1.7 trillion dollars, or about 50% while another one-third comes from your payroll taxes. Prior to the Trump tax cuts, corporations only paid 9% of the federal income taxes collected, and that will now drop to 7%. Those poor corporations, they had it rough. As a matter of fact those corporations have it so rough they actually hide over two trillion dollars in cash overseas. It blows my mind how greedy people who run corporations are. Don't worry though because when the Democrats with the Presidency again they will reverse these disgusting corporate tax cuts for sure! As a matter of fact according to a June 29th 2020 article by CNBC, and my own ears because I've heard it myself Joe Biden told potential donors to his campaign that he would roll back most of President Donald Trump's multi trillion dollar tax cuts, even though "a lot of you may not like that." So when President Joe Biden signed the "Inflation Reduction Act" into law surely he must have repealed the Trump tax cuts. Give me a second, I'm just going to double check and see how President Biden went about smashing those tax cuts for the wealthy. Oh boy, oh man, damn it! The Democrats got us again! In passing the Inflation Reduction Act the Democrats completely left the 2017 Tax Cuts and Jobs Act intact. The Democrats love to let the Republicans do their bidding for them so they can blame them and still pretend to be on the side of the middle class.

Gas, and Oil companies get huge tax breaks for basically looking for, and drilling for the very product they sell. That would be like incentivizing McDonald's to search for cows for their hamburgers. U.S. taxpayers subsidize the oil, and gas industry's business from the start to the finish. In 2016 Exxonmobil received a $406 million income tax benefit! It's disgusting, and we can actually go back to Bill Clinton's Presidency to when he signed the DeepWater Royalty Relief Act. This act waived the 12% royalty fee Big Oil would have owed once they found oil off our Gulf Coast. Again though Trump's cult members and many others are mad at a single mother getting some help, but don't seem to mind the billions going to corporate welfare.

In the end the Trump tax cuts will help himself, and other wealthy individuals now and into the future much more than it will ever help the middle class. An average middle class family will only save about $1,000.00 on their taxes, and as mentioned earlier, the tax cut for the middle class expires in 2026. A family in the top 1% would save approximately $215,000 while a family who are in the top 0.1% would save over 1 million dollars. I know you're thinking, "well they pay more so they are going to save more, so who cares?" Well, in my opinion they don't need to have any tax savings. When someone earns enormous sums of money they can pay higher taxes. It's for the betterment of our entire country, and individuals, and corporations have to stop being so selfish and greedy.

Trump signed 96 Laws in his first year. Can you imagine if he knew Obama signed 124 Laws in his first year? Trump would have signed anything to get to 125. President Trump being the consistent liar he is stated in a speech to first responders in West Palm Beach, Florida "We have more legislation passed, including the record- was Harry Truman. That's a long time ago. And we broke that record. So we have a lot done." Well, unless you're counting Obama, Bush, Clinton, H.W. Bush, Reagan, Carter, Nixon, Kennedy and Eisenhower. One thing President Trump truly has excelled at is telling lies. The Washington Post had President Trump making 3,001 untrue statements at the time I first wrote this. Now in the Washington Post's August 1st, 2018 article, the Post has President Trump making 4,229 false or misleading claims in 558 days in office. That is an average of almost 8 lies or misleading statements each and every day! I've been debating on putting many of President Trump's lies in here, but I suppose Trump's lies would take about 20 or 30 pages alone. Instead, in honor of David Letterman I think I will do a top 10 list. I was a big Letterman fan back when he was at the top of his game.

Number 10. "The overall audience was, I think, the biggest ever to watch an inauguration address, which was a great thing." (Sorry, estimates are put at about 600,000 ouch, you lost to Obama again who had about 1.8 million). **Number 9.**"I never said Russia did not meddle in the election, I said 'it may be Russia, or China (Jina, Jina, ☺) or another country or group, or it may be a 400 pound genius sitting in bed, and playing with his computer." (Trump called it "Fake News" and in an interview with Time Magazine, President Trump stated "I don't believe they interfered"). **Number 8.** "The 2018 defense authorization bill includes raises for the military for the first time in 10 years." (I only wish this were true). **Number 7.** "In many places, like California the same person votes many times. You probably heard about that. They always like to say 'oh that's a conspiracy theory.' Not a conspiracy theory, folks. Millions, and millions of people." (It was two people Donald; Beavis and Butthead, you dumbass). **Number 6.** "Terrible! Just found out that Obama had my 'wires tapped' in Trump Tower just before the victory. Nothing found. This is McCarthyism!" (All the racist Obama haters still probably believe that bs). **Number 5.** "Obamacare covers very few people." (Only if you consider approximately 10 million people in 2017 a few people). **Number 4.** "Nobody knows if Russia interfered with the election" (unless you count everybody). **Number 3.** "With the exception of the late, great Abraham Lincoln, I can be more presidential than any president that's ever held this office." (I know that's an opinion, but we all know Larry the Cable Guy would be more Presidential than Trump's utterly embarrassing, joke of a Presidency). **Number 2.** "We are going to repeal, and replace Obamacare, quickly, easily, on day one." (The President and the GOP has relentlessly attempted to repeal Obamacare. Republicans have made over 70 failed attempts). (Mostly prior to the Trump Presidency). **Number 1. "Fake News!!!!"** (Every scandal, every lie, it's all made up according to the Donald. Although, in all honesty, much of the news we hear is all to close to "fake news". The news organizations all lie, put their spin on the news or fail to report news they don't like. I find Fox News is often willing to just make stuff up out of the clear, thin blue air, whereas the CNN's and MSNBCs of the world either put their spin on the news or just fail to report news. Both are horrible and if anyone thinks we live in a country that has free press you are as delusional as President Trump was. We have corporate sponsored news. The Covid coverage brought to you by Pfizer, Johnon and

Johnson and Moderna is a great example and I'll cover that much more in the Covid Conspiracy's chapter. President Trump's cult followers were and most still are only all too happy to fall in line, and believe him, even when they heard or seen it for themselves.) **Top 10 Bonus-** "Barack Obama was working with the head of a Muslim drug cartel. They have them, they don't tell you, but I assure you they do, and they are even bigger than the Mexican cartels. Barack made millions while he was President, he did, and I have proof, and I will show everyone along with his real birth certificate very soon." (Okay, he didn't actually say that.........Yet).

Trump consistently spoke during his campaign about how he was going to "drain the swamp" and like most anything that comes out of Trump's mouth, it is complete bullshit. Washington lobbyists who are the epitome of the swamp are doing as well or better than ever. According to statista.com, $3.37 billion were spent lobbying in 2017. That's right, $3.37 billion, with the influential NRA spending $5.1 million making sure assault rifles are readily available to anyone who would like to have a mass shooting of their own under their belt. The team President Trump assembled to advise him with his tax reform plan, and who are or were in key positions in the Trump White House, include former Goldman Sachs executives Steve Mnunchin, Gary Cohen, Dina Powell and Steve Bannon. Steve Bannon was banished, and I would imagine is sitting in his basement, not having showered in months, rubbing an AR-15 while plotting his revenge. Gary Cohen resigned as Director of the National Economic Council. Top national security adviser Dina Powell resigned, and returned to the open arms of Goldman Sachs as a partner in the Investment Banking Division while Trump defender, and Chief Economic Adviser Steve Mnunchin remains in the swamp, swimming around with the Donald. The biggest joke of all when it comes to doing the exact opposite of draining the swamp is the head of the EPA, Swamp King, Scott Pruitt. This guy is a walking nightmare for both our tax dollars, and the environment. In his life as an asshole prior to being put on as the head of the EPA, Pruitt consistently, and loudly called for the elimination of the agency he now heads. In a 2015 Fox Fake News interview, Pruitt stated the "environment would be just fine without the EPA."

Trump knew that in Pruitt he would get the pro-pollution, pro-business, anti-environmental protection person he wanted to undo any pesky laws that limit corporations from polluting our earth. As Oklahoma's attorney general that jackass, Scott Pruitt, sued the EPA 13 times. Yeah, that's the guy we need to head our EPA. More than likely this isn't actually Trump's fault. It honestly could be as simple as no one actually told Trump what the letters "EPA" even stand for. Knowledge is the key to solving any problem, and when someone in charge lacks in-depth knowledge on any, and all subjects he is left to be guided by his greedy and selfish nature. According to the watchdog group American Oversight, Mr. Pruitt has, or is attempting to weaken, or eliminate many environmental protections. Pruitt vacated the planned ban of neurotoxic agriculture pesticide, "chlorpyrifos," which causes brain damage in children. Pruitt rolled back the Clean Power Plan to reduce pollution from coal fired power plants. We all know how Trump loves coal. Pruitt's campaigns, and political organizations received contributions from Clean Power Plan opponents including $25,000 from the coal company Murray Energy. Mr. Pruitt directed staff to scrub decades of climate change data from the EPA website, and got rid of any independent scientific advisors because "Science" is no friend to Mr. Pruitt's EPA.

In protest, and defiance to Mr. Pruitt, more than 700 EPA staff members have since left the agency they once worked for.

Lastly, Swamp King Scott Pruitt's money, and pay for play scandals are almost as much of a daily story as Trump's marital affairs. Pruitt has spent millions of dollars on a 20 member, full time security staff detail that is more than three times the size of his predecessor's part-time security team. Swamp King, Scott Pruitt spent $43,000 for a soundproof booth, and no one knows why, including Mr. Pruitt. Mr. Pruitt also authorized large raises for two close aides, and to this day it does not seem Mr. Pruitt has followed through on his promise to rescind the raises. Mr. Pruitt, along with his security, flies first class, and has used both private planes, and military jets to travel. The perks didn't stop with travel either. Mr. Pruitt lived in an expensive Capitol Hill condo owned by a healthcare lobbyist. For some reason Mr. Pruitt paid far, far less than the fair market value. Mr. Pruitt used his expensive security detail on trips to Disneyland, the Rose Bowl and Italy. Scott "the Swamp King " Pruitt travels around first class like he is a real king, and he is; Mr. Pruitt is definitely the "Swamp King". Congratulations Mr. Pruitt, and congratulations President Trump on another bullshit, un-kept promise. There were many other swamp creatures who swam around in the Trump administration.

Urban Development Secretary and Professional SleepWalker Ben Carson got himself into a little hot water after attempting to buy a dining set for $31,000. Like most married men, Ben originally tried to blame his wife, but internal agency emails showed both himself, and his wife were aware and helped in selecting the furniture. I'm not sure if the entire White House is in rough shape or not, but 23 agencies have spent considerable amounts of money on renovations. Mr. Tom Price, who was President Trump's first Secretary of Health and Human Services was fired in just over a half a year of service after apparently spending approximately $1 million in federal funds on private jet travel. It seems Trump's entire administration treats the government, and our tax dollars like we are their wealthy father, and they are our spoiled rich brats. Creepy Secretary Steve Mnunchin spent over $800,000 on seven flights he took using military aircraft. "Dad, I'm going to have Captain Frost fly me in one of the military planes. You know how I hate people." I think I'm starting to understand why Trump makes up these names for people. It's kind of fun; Swamp King Scott Pruitt, Creepy Steve Mnunchin, Sleepwalking Ben Carson.

Trump won big with poor, uneducated, white voters, and it will be interesting if the policies that Trump, and the GOP are putting in place which will clearly hurt his rural voters will end up hurting him. I was wrong, it wasn't interesting and his policies didn't hurt his popularity with poor,white voters one bit. I've found facts mean little to the Trump voter so this was not exactly a surprise. President Trump can implement policies, and then just blame Obama, and they will probably believe him. Trump understands it's not what he does, but it's the feelings he creates by the things he says. The only reason that type of thinking may get Trump in trouble this time is because they will have a feeling of hunger in their bellies. In the last election those voters listened to their hearts, now in order for Trump to win their votes they may have to listen to their heads, and not their hearts. Which one will win out? President Trump has started a bit of a trade war which could bring about tariffs on our exporting U.S. crops. China would put tariffs on pork, tobacco, and soybeans. Planned cuts in agricultural subsidies (Which, depending on how that would look I could be in favor of). What I would not be in favor of is cuts to food stamps, and work requirements which would hurt food stamp recipients who live in rural areas. I think many white Trump voters assume it's lazy minorities who are stealing all the money from good, working, white people. Sorry Trumpsters, but working class whites make up the largest block of government funded poverty-reduction programs. Over 6 million whites benefit from government safety net programs, while African Americans represent just under 3 million, Hispanics about 2.5 million and "Other" representing about 700,000. Whites receive about 36% of all food stamps, African Americans about 26%, Hispanics about 17%. The remainder goes to "other" or "unknown." The extremely costly Medicaid program has over 40% of the benefactors being white, a little less than 20% being black, about 17% Hispanic and the rest coming from my favorite and the sometimes used by yours truly category of "Other." Okay, since this isn't Fox Fake News I'm going to shed a little light on those numbers here, and make white people feel better. They say numbers don't lie, but they certainly can bend the truth, or at least be put out in a way that doesn't tell the whole truth. The Census Bureau measures who the recipients are of six government programs which include Medicaid, food stamps, housing assistance, supplemental Security Income (SSI), Temporary Assistance for Needy Families (TANF) and General Assistance. 42% of African Americans received at least one of these benefits, 36% of Hispanics, 18% of Asians/Pacific Islanders and 13% of non-Hispanic Whites. There are many factors as to why African Americans have the highest poverty rate, but I will write more about that in my section about race.

One of Trump's worst nominations was his nomination of an angry leprechaun named Jeff Sessions. The Attorney General was hell bent, with God on his side, at continuing, and enhancing the government's war on drugs. Sessions overturned the DOJ's policy instructing prosecutors not to specify drug amounts when filing charges against low level, non-violent offenders. Sessions would like to go after marijuana growers, and distributors in states where it is legal, thus flexing the federal government's power over state rights. Now this little angry leprechaun is tearing families apart, and separating children from their parents as they enter the country illegally or even in cases where they enter legally seeking asylum. Sessions gleefully stood before the cameras, and used the bible for justification for this policy. Isn't it strange how those who proclaim to love Jesus the most act in the complete opposite manner Jesus acted? Trump is shamefully using children as bargaining chips to try and get financing for his border wall from the Democrats. Wait, I thought Mexico was paying for that? Trump seems to be happy with Sessions at the moment, but we all know like any Trump marriage, it won't last. Hopefully Trump's disdain for Sessions over his handling of the Russia probe will motivate Trump even more to possibly legalize marijuana at the federal level. I know legalization of marijuana is wishful thinking at this point, even under a Democrat. However, the legalization is inevitable, and it's not just because public opinion is for the legalization of marijuana. In the end the thing that will push the legalization of marijuana over the top is corporations getting involved, and spreading the money around to buy the right politicians.

The good news is Trump dislikes Sessions, and regrets nominating him as his AG in the first place, so maybe he will fire him after all. Feel free to call Mr. Sessions an "Angry Leprechaun" Mr. President. Sure enough the marriage to AG Jeff Sessions ended in divorce as I thought it would. Sessions was fired by Trump and replaced with loyalist Matthew G. Whitaker.

I think I could keep going on and on about many of the things wrong with President Trump. I think as a country nothing surprises us anymore as to what we see Trump do, hear Trump say, or read Trump tweet. The problem is too much of the country loves it. We have an "us versus them" dynamic that is impossible to get out of now. Trump supporters are so entrenched on that side of things a fact is completely unrecognizable to them. It's become personal to Trump's supporters. Any criticism of Trump is a criticism of them personally. Now Trump is indicted and I believe the indictment will make Trump's supporters just dig in more. So what do we do?

Conclusion

These numbers seem to fluctuate slightly but, in general about 25% of the country supports Trump no matter what. There is also going to be a small percentage of the country that is going to vote Republican because they are easily fooled, and distracted by the social issues which they are aligned with on the Republican side. There is also another small percentage that is aligned with the Republican Party, and traditionally that's who they vote for no matter what. Oh, and of course many, extremely wealthy individuals vote Republicanand and seeing as the Republicans enable you to avoid paying your share of taxes I understand why you would vote Republican.

Then we have a percentage of the country that is going to vote with or for the Democratic Party. Approximately 31% of the country identifies as Democrats or at least lean Democratic compared to 29% of the country who identify as Republicans with the largest percentage of the country identifying as independents (38%). I won't get into the breakdown of race, gender, etc. because I do not think that's necessary. The problem is the perception that we can only have a viable candidate from these two parties. They are both corrupt, and work almost completely for corporations interest. Are there differences between the two parties? Sure, the Republicans want to give corporations 99.9% of all the wealth in the country while the Democrats want to only give the corporations about 98.9% leaving us all with a few more crumbs.

I did think the Trump administration brought out the differences between the two parties more than ever, but now I'm not so sure. To be clear though I believe the Republicans are brutal, cold hearted, greedy, hate-filled bastards. The Democrats just aren't much better, but the Democrats do understand they can't lock you out in the cold completely. The Democrats certainly have more compassion for those without or at least want their votes. The Democrats understand they need to throw you something, while the Republicans blatantly want it all! In the end though, the thing is, we are sick of choosing the lesser of two evils. That's partly what happened in the 2016 election. We wanted the best option, which was Bernie Sanders. When the Democratic Party stole that option for us, and tried to sell the argument of Hillary still being much better than Trump, we weren't buying it. Unfortunately when the exact same scenario happened with Bernie and Biden the public did buy the Democrats bullshit and elected Biden, the lesser of the two evils. I mean with Hillary we were fairly certain she would be the better option, but like I said earlier, fuck the Democrats, and fuck Hillary and now after what will be 4 more years of broken promises and blaming the Republicans, fuck Joey B too.

The whole corrupt two party system deserves one big fuck you from all of us. So many of us are so easily distracted by the bullshit social issues while they` continually rob us all blind. The Democrats are every bit as complicit in the corrupt system itself as the Republicans are. What I mean by that is, the Democrats bow to corporate interests. The Democrats work for Wall Street, for the Military Industrial complex, for the prison industrial complex, for the pharmaceutical industry, and although they are the lesser of the two evils we all deserve better. As a country we have to get out of the mindset that there are only two options.

I voted for Jill Stein in the 2016 election in hopes that she would garnish enough votes to start changing the two party narrative. Whose fault is it we cannot get a serious third party candidate? It is absolutely the national media's fault. We need to demand they give other candidates and parties equal coverage. The 2016 election produced the two most unpopular candidates in the history of our country. *In the history of our country,* and yet we couldn't find a viable third party candidate? In 1992 Ross Perot got 19% of the popular vote, but Mr. Perot had to fight tooth, and nail to be included into the debates. Since the 1992 debates not one third party candidate has been allowed to participate again. The media locks any other candidate out, refuses to give them any coverage, and when they do, the media never fails to keep reminding us all that the individual has no chance in hell of winning. Without adequate media coverage it's impossible for a third party candidate to break into the national consciousness. If Jill Stein was given proper coverage I have no doubt she could have competed with the two worst candidates in the history of the world. There was so much to dislike about

Hillary, Biden and Trump; Jill Stein would have looked like a gift candidate. I'm not a Gary Johnson fan, because in all honesty he didn't seem too bright so that's why I'm not mentioning him as much as Jill Stein. Although, Mr. Johnson is for the legalization of marijuana, so there's one positive. Why not have a debate with 3 candidates? That needs to be the new norm. It would be the Republican candidate, the Democratic candidate, and whichever other Party's candidate is pulling the highest. If the media gave them equal coverage, and Americans became accustomed to having three or four choices then we wouldn't have a President Trump. I understand that sometimes we may get a President who much of the country dislikes, but with the exception of President Obama I don't recall having a choice for President where I felt yes, that should be our leader. The bottom line is we have to unite, get rid of the two party system that often resembles a one party system, and give the country more choices. Let's make America a true Democracy.

Chapter-2

A Judicial Joke

America's criminal justice system is the ultimate hypocrisy of America. It is nothing more than an immoral jobs program that crushes individual's lives, and tears families apart. I didn't want to, but I guess I have no choice here, but to start with my own story. I was arrested for armed robbery along with my best friend Wared (Wadi) Abdellatif and Bobby Vitagliano. Myself and Wadi pled "not guilty", and went to trial while Bobby Vitagliano turned government witness, and testified against myself, and Wared Abdellatif. The federal government has a 98% conviction rate so the odds were stacked against us. I also had a couple of other charges stemming from the original charge including conspiracy to transport interstate commerce, and a witness tampering charge. The witness tampering charge was due to a stupid, inappropriate email to an ex-girlfriend where I stated I wasn't going to jail for something I didn't do, and if she testified I was going to have to tell my lawyer everything I knew about her to discredit her. I should have never written the e-mail, but there was nothing I could do once it was sent. AOL, which was the email of choice back then had an awesome "un-send" option. Unfortunately, I used yahoo mail, and when I realized I made a mistake, and I went to un-send the email, regrettably that option was not available.

The trial was prosecuted by an immoral, piece of shit prosecutor, Anthony Bruce. Mr. Bruce, like most prosecutors, is only concerned with numbers. Mr. Bruce has come under fire many times for his unethical behavior. The judge in the case was a real piece of work as well, and I often wondered who was in charge of the trial, the judge or the prosecutor? That piece of garbage's name is Richard Arcara. Judge Arcara would often fall asleep during the trial, but since in the end the prosecutor was the only one Judge Arcara was going to listen to, I guess Judge Arcara figured it didn't matter if he slept. It's my belief that all federal and state judges are pieces of garbage because they participate, and profit from our immoral criminal justice system. The trial itself had its ups and downs, but I felt pretty good about everything going into closing arguments. The night before, the jury came back with a verdict; a report was sent to the judge stating it was 11 to 1, but one person wouldn't change their mind, and needed to hear more evidence. I thought we were fucked, and not in the good way, but luckily I was wrong. Eleven of the jurors wanted to find both of us not guilty, with one juror wanting to find myself guilty of the witness tampering charge. Guilty of a witness tampering charge for a crime they found me not guilty of. It didn't even make sense, but in the email I mentioned I would have to tell my lawyer my ex suffered from bi-polar disorder. Possibly this one juror may have suffered from mental illness herself, and she took what I wrote personally, and thus would not give in.

The jury thought I would get a slap on the wrist, meaning probation so I was told that was one of the reasons they gave in to the lone juror. The guideline for the witness tampering charge carried a 10 to 16 month sentence. Even though for an e-mail a 10 to 16 month sentence would be excessive, the sentence I received turned out to be much worse. In the federal system they can take acquitted conduct into account, and enhance your sentence outside your guideline range. In other words the judge can sentence you for conduct a jury of your peers found you Not Guilty of. When I tell my friends that 2/3rd's of my sentence was based on conduct I was found not guilty of, I can tell they almost don't believe me, or at least feel I have something wrong. They say, "No, they can't do that" well, one thing I've learned is "they" get to do anything they want. The rules only apply to the defendants. The judge, who is on the same team as the prosecutor, determines your guilt by a bullshit standard called a "preponderance of the evidence."

If you think the judge is a neutral party, you're sadly mistaken. Your sentence is actually determined for the most part by the prosecutor, and a probation officer. The probation officer with the help of the prosecutor writes a pre-sentence report recommending a sentence to the judge. The guideline range they put me into taking into account my acquitted conduct was much higher than the 10-16 month sentence I should have received. I walked out of sentencing that day with a 48 month sentence.

I went to prison feeling confident I would win my appeal. I remember meeting a guy in prison named Freddy. I don't remember his last name, but what I do remember was what he told me. Mr. Freddy said, you will never win because once they give you a number, they never let you go. I was still very naïve on what a joke our criminal justice system is, so I was certain I would win. As a part of the appeal we even obtained a letter from one of the jurors stating that all but one juror wanted to find me not guilty of the witness tampering charge, but they all compromised with that one juror to find me guilty even though they did not think I was guilty of the witness tampering. As a matter of fact the piece of shit FBI agent who got my ex fiance to testify against me was the individual who did the real threatening. According to my ex, he was screaming at her, and told her she was going to be arrested and thrown in jail if she didn't sign a statement against me. Then the FBI agent wrote out the statement, and my ex-girlfriend signed it.

During sentencing my lawyer brought up this fact as it was also revealed at trial, and the scumbag, piece of shit judge played dumb and senile, and refused to even acknowledge what my lawyer was saying. Judge Richard Arcara kept repeating "What are you saying?" "What do you mean?" he would never give an answer, and finally my lawyer became frustrated, and moved on from the issue. The judge, the prosecutor, the FBI, they were all dirty liars. The FBI even went so far as to have evidence destroyed that would have easily changed the outcome of the trial and possibly prohibited the government from even bringing about any charges. A childhood friend of mine who while growing up was like another brother to me was a police officer for the Niagara Falls Police Department. He informed me the night of the robbery three young men were pulled over and ski masks were found in their car. He was going to get me the police report and that would have halted everything. However, when he went to get the report it no longer existed and he informed me the FBI had a few meetings with the higher ups and he was certain the FBI had the report destroyed as a favor. It's disgusting behavior but it's typical of law enforcement. The appeal was filed, and I went to prison hoping to be home in about a year. I didn't know the appeals process was a complete farce. The news that I had lost my appeal was a difficult day. It was one of the two hardest days I had in prison. My first difficult day came about one week into my sentence. My sister Marni was going to visit her husband Frank's family who lived fairly close to the prison. She brought her kids with her who I was very close with. I used to always stop by my sisters on the way home to see my nephew Austin, and my nieces Madison, Kelsi and Regan. Kelsi and Regan were both really young and were hanging on me as usual and happy as can be with really no idea I was in prison. As they left they were waving at me not knowing this would be the last time I would see them for some time. I knew though and it broke my heart. In prison you're always alone, yet you're never alone so it's tough to find a place where you can sort of grieve over a situation. In general I'm not someone who cries and I've only cried maybe twice in my adult life, but this took everything I had not to completely break down. I soon found something to pour myself into, and feel like I was able to fight back some. I started working on my own appeal called a 2255 Writ of Habeas Corpus. It's a civil appeal, and I truly loved doing the research, and putting together the appeal. I think I came up with 15 arguments, and a few were very promising. The judge has no time limit on when he has to look at and decide your appeal by, so it should not have shocked me that my scumbag judge waited until I was close to going home before denying my appeal. However, I did have a few issues that I appealed to the New York State Supreme Court and I actually won on a conflict of interest issue. A few lawyers told me the decision in my case was spoken about everywhere. With the court system being a farce though, the State court remanded the case back to Judge Arcara who obviously would never rule in my favor. So we went through the motions, and Judge Arcara denied the appeal, and the State Supreme Court let him have that final decision so I'm not sure why they even bothered.

I won't get into the details of the conflict of interest because it's not important. The issue that is important, and that should bother everyone is the fact my sentence was almost in its entirety based on conduct that a jury of my peers found me not guilty of. In my Habeas Corpus appeal there was an interesting case before the United States Supreme Court that gave me hope. Actually, I was watching this particular case early on in my sentence, and when CNN reported how the case had been decided I almost started jumping up and down. I started making phone calls telling people based on this decision I should be going home ASAP. Again though, I was naïve, I had no idea what a farce the whole system is, and that God himself could not get you out of the federal system once you're in it. The case I'm referring to was Blakely v. Washington. Ralph Howard Blakely kidnapped his estranged wife in an attempt to remarry her. Mr. Blakely's idea for winning his wife back wasn't exactly romantic, but to each his or her own. Mr. Blakely kidnapped his wife, and forced her into a wooden box in the back of his pickup truck all while making his 13 year old son follow behind his mom and dad in another car with the threat of having his mother shot if he did not do as he was told. Mr. Blakely was originally charged with first-degree kidnapping, but in exchange for saving the state taxpayers the unnecessary tax burden of going to trial, Mr. Blakely agreed to plead guilty to second degree kidnapping which carried a guideline range of 49 to 53 months in prison. The judge, finding that Blakely acted with "deliberate cruelty" imposed a sentence of 90 months. Blakely appealed his sentence as it violated his Sixth Amendment right to an impartial jury trial citing Apprendi v. New Jersey. Apprendi v. New Jersey was a Supreme Court case where the justices struck down state laws which allowed judges rather than juries to decide between life in prison or the death penalty. Blakely followed the same logic as Apprendi, and argued only a jury of his peers could find the extra sentencing decision, and that decision would have to be made under the "beyond a reasonable doubt" standard I think we all would want. The Supreme Court ruled, and applied their ruling in Apprendi in which it stated "Other than the fact of a prior conviction, any fact that increases the penalty for a crime beyond the prescribed statutory maximum must be submitted to a jury, and proved beyond a reasonable doubt." Justice Scalia went on to write that the Apprendi rule ensures that "the judge's authority to sentence derives wholly from the jury's verdict. Without that restriction, the jury would not exercise the control that the Framers intended."

In case you're confused at all at this point, part of the factors being considered by the Justices are the guidelines, and the statutory maximum. The "statutory maximum for a particular crime may be 10 years, 20 years, etc. An individual can be offered a deal to plead guilty and then the individual would be put in one of many guideline ranges. If he admitted to certain factors he may fall into a 10 to 16 month guideline, or some other guideline range. In this particular case the facts that Blakely admitted to, put him into a guideline range of 49 to 53 months. At this point in time the guidelines were mandatory. Whether you were found guilty by a jury of your peers or you plead guilty, the facts of what you were found guilty of, or what you plead guilty to would put an individual into a particular guideline range. As a defendant, if you plead guilty, the biggest determining factor for you to make that decision is the guideline range you would fall into. Let's pretend you were charged in a crime which had a 10 year statutory maximum. If you thought the judge might impose a 9 ½ year sentence you may as well roll the dice and go to trial. However, if the state or federal government offers to put you into a 49 to 53 month guideline range in exchange for not going to trial, you would be motivated to take that deal. In Justice

O'Connor's dissenting opinion the Justice feared or foresaw that in applying Apprendi to the sentencing guidelines, traditional sentencing factors would have to be charged in the indictment, and proved to a jury beyond a reasonable doubt. Yeah, no shit you asshole. That is exactly the way every American thinks this shit is being done in the first place!

Here's the problem with everyone being on the same team, and the defendant being out there by himself: You could have 19 charges against you with a small, insignificant charge thrown in with the more serious charges. The jury could then find you not guilty of 18 out of the 19 charges. That one charge may carry a 10 to 16 month sentence, but the judge could enhance the defendant's sentence for each charge, and as long as he stays under the 20 year statutory sentence he's fine. This exact scenario happened to a defendant while I was appealing my sentence. This poor guy was found not guilty on 18 out of his 19 charges. He ended up in the same 10 to 16 month guideline range as I did, but this poor bastard got a 19-year sentence! After I read about that case, I could not even complain about mine aloud any more. Nobody knows about this bullshit, and nobody cares about this bullshit until it happens to him or her or someone they love.

After the Blakey v. Washington decision; prosecutors, and judges throughout the country were in a sheer panic mood. It was insane! The Supreme Court has lifetime appointees so sometimes many of the Justices are actually unaware of what's going on in the lower courts. What was going on was the lower courts had been fucking over defendants left and right with these enhancements for years. The enhancements are determined by the prosecutor, the pre-sentence report, which is written by a probation officer at the direction of the prosecutor, and the judge who rubber stamps it. Now, just as I was excited at the prospect of having my sentence reduced to the 10 to 16 month sentence guideline range that the jury conviction should have put me into, as were many other defendants. Even more importantly, the corrupt criminal justice system needs to lock people up for long periods of time, and there are two things they depend upon: Prosecutors and judges count on enhancements not proved to a jury, and snitches. The government banks on giving defendants longer sentences, especially if you have the nerve to plead not guilty, and go to trial. The entire court system was literally going crazy! I'm sure many talks took place in private to let the Justices know what has been going on in the lower courts. Once the Supreme Court was made aware of the fact that thousands and thousands of people had been sentenced for crimes they were found not guilty of, nor plead guilty to the Supreme Court; then agreed to review two cases involving the constitutionality of the sentence enhancements under the federal guidelines. Due to the urgency of the many sweaty prosecutors and judges the Supreme Court ordered the briefs in Booker to be submitted in September 2004, and oral arguments would take place on October 4th. The court's decision came out on January 12th 2005. Although the actual decision had been made behind closed doors months before by immoral prosecutors and judges pleading with the Justices to save their disgusting, corrupt system. The justice system, the country, and their jobs all depend upon it. So here's what these Supreme assholes did: The Supreme Court stated Booker was indeed correct. Mr. Booker's sixth amendment right to a jury trial had been violated. We won!!! Not so fast Mr. Booker and everyone else who were sentenced for crimes they were found not guilty of. We are taking our time here in fucking with you, and then fucking you, call it foreplay if you will. Justice

Stevens wrote "As the Blakely court found in Apprendi v. New Jersey, the 'statutory maximum' sentence a judge may impose solely on the basis of the facts reflected in the jury verdict or admitted by the defendant." There is no constitutional difference between the guidelines, and the statutory maximum. Be patient Mr. Blakely, we love foreplay. "Were the Guidelines merely advisory –recommending, but not requiring, the selection of particular sentences in response to differing sets of facts- their use would not implicate the Sixth Amendment. However, that is not the case. Title 18 U.S.C. A. 3553 (b) directs that a court "shall impose a sentence of the kind, and within the range." Established by the Guidelines, subject to departures in specific, limited cases. Because they are binding on all judges, this Court has consistently held that the Guidelines have the force and effect of laws. So listen Mr. Blakely with all this being said, I'm going to let Justice Breyer come in and have some fun with you as well. Don't worry though, Justice Breyer doesn't really like foreplay like I do. Justice Breyer is going to come in, and just fuck you. This will not feel good, but unfortunately it will be memorable in all the wrong ways.

Fuck away Justice...... "18 U.S.C. A.3553 (b) (1) which makes the Federal Sentencing Guidelines mandatory, is incompatible with today's Sixth Amendment "jury trial" holding and therefore must be severed and excised from the Sentencing Reform Act of 1984 (Act). Section 3742 €, which depends upon the Guidelines' mandatory nature, also must be severed and excised. So modified, the Act makes the Guidelines effectively advisory, requiring a sentencing court to consider Guidelines ranges, see 3553 (a) (4), but permitting it to tailor the sentence in light of the other statutory concerns." The Justices made it clear that courts should still sentence within the guidelines taking into account "circumstances for departure." In other words, the Justices knew what was taking place violated our constitutional rights; but once the Justices were informed of what was happening in the real world, the Justices changed the mandatory guidelines to advisory; eliminating the "shall" apply verbiage. Each Justice should be utterly ashamed of themselves. Every Congressman, and Senator should be ashamed of themselves as well.

For me, learning everything I was taught was bullshit was nothing less than heart breaking. If you hardly know anything of the constitution growing up, one of the phrases a person is usually familiar with is; the right to a trial by a jury of their peers. To learn that the government takes that basic constitutional right and spits on it, crushed me. I have no respect for most judges, and maybe even less for most prosecutors. For prosecutors it's a numbers game. They rely on snitches, and they don't care what the snitch did as long as he or she gives them more people to lock up. Take Sammy "the Bull" Gravano who confessed to 19 murders, and was given a 5 year sentence just because he cooperated with the government. Some ninety prosecutors, and investigators wrote letters commending Gravano for his help. John Gleeson, the lead prosecutor in the John Gotti trial, characterized Gravano as the most significant witness in the history of organized crime. I guess that's true considering Gravano's testimony helped imprison 36 of his former mob associates. The FBI's Jim Fox presented Gravano with an award reserved for agents who show uncommon valor which was a specially designed wristwatch with an American flag on its face. Judge Glasser believed Gravano had changed from a murdering gangster to a law and order advocate. I guess that didn't turn out to be the case because in 2000 Gravano was arrested, and indicted in an ecstasy ring that grossed $500,000.00 a week. One of the problems with rats is just like people who are tortured, you cannot depend on their testimony to be truthful. A rat will say anything to get out of trouble. Cooperating with the government is truly the only possible way to get a downward departure. When I was in prison you always knew if someone was a snitch because they would make up some bullshit story of why the judge was lenient on him. I remember this one guy telling his story and saying how the judge liked him and thought he deserved a second chance so he gave him a year when his guideline was closer to six years. Nope, sorry, you told and I know it. Go tell that bs to another snitch because they are the only ones you're fooling. The problem for rats is because they were a snitch they had no idea that you can't get less than the guidelines unless you cooperated.

Take rapper T.I. who was arrested on federal gun charges hours before he was set to perform on the BET Hip Hop Awards show. T.I. who is a convicted felon, bought three machine guns in a sting operation that involved one of his bodyguards who was a rat himself. Investigators found three more firearms in the car which T.I. drove to pick up the machine guns and silencers. Being a felon caught with any gun you are looking at an automatic five years, (per gun) add in that the guns were machine guns and then silencers which opens up a whole other can of worms - T.I. was looking at some serious time. Somehow, T.I. only received a sentence of a year and one day. The prosecutor stated T.I. was in a unique position to perform community service. The only community service T.I. performed was telling on everyone, and anyone he knew anything about. I can't even imagine how many people T.I. snitched on in order to get the year-and-a-day sentence he received. I love rap, and I was a T.I. fan, but now I have to turn the station if I hear him rap.

T.I. makes me sick, and I can't believe all the rappers out there who I'm sure have guys they grew up with doing serious time, and they still kick it with T.I. knowing he had to snitch to get that bullshit sentence. One of the CD's I listen to often is Biggie Duets, and T.I. raps a verse that goes "real niggers is doing their time, they ain't here, you commit the same crime come home the same year". Yeah you sure did you fucking rat. T.I. is still probably cooperating with the federal government, so if you're doing dirt in the ATL, watch out, because T.I. is taking notes. If you are wondering why I wrote about T.I. it's because the theme of this book is hypocrisy, and here he is talking that tough shit, but when it comes down to it, like most people he was soft as cotton.

Walking around the prison yard and staring at a 25 foot barbed wire fence isn't easy. You have to be mentally tough to take that. Being locked up does something to your soul, but as a man I always knew while I was walking around that I could do life if I had to. I certainly would not want to do life in prison, but the decision to rat on someone or to not rat on someone has to be made for yourself. Times have changed. At one time, especially being Italian, if you were a rat you were ostracized from your community. I always think of the line in "A Bronx Tale" where Calogero says "I didn't rat dad, I didn't rat." Then, while thinking to himself he says "All I knew was, a rat was the lowest thing anyone could be in my neighborhood, and I didn't rat". It's not the way it is anymore though, therefore you have to not be a rat for yourself. For me, I could never rat someone out, and live with myself. When my father grew up as a young guy in Niagara Falls the mob was still big, and I think that was a value in the streets back then, and luckily for me he passed that value onto me.

I don't think very many policies have had more of a negative effect on poor communities, and especially on African Americans than the war on drugs. I'm trying to stay away from bombarding the reader here with a bunch of stats that end up not meaning much. When someone throws around too many stats it starts to skew the point they were actually trying to make. Emotion drives people to do something; facts and statistics just don't have the effect they should. A quote that comes to mind is "The death of one man is a tragedy. The death of a million is a statistic." Joseph Stalin I will have to start out with some here though, and then sprinkle a decent amount throughout, sorry. The American criminal justice system holds approximately 2.3 million people, with 1 out of every 5 people being incarcerated for a drug offense. To be honest I thought the number would be much higher. Well, actually it is; turns out if you get arrested for a drug offense as well as a more serious offense the crime is reported for the most serious offense only. According to the BOP (Bureau of Prisons) 46.2% of federal prisoners are incarcerated for drug offenses, and the number is even higher in the State system.

As I wrote about earlier, I believe the criminal justice system is nothing more than an immoral jobs program. For every 100 people locked up there are approximately 35 jobs created; lock up another 100 people, 35 more jobs, lock up 100 more, 35 more jobs. Tying up individuals in the criminal justice system not only creates jobs, but it also takes millions out of the job market. I believe that's one of the reasons for the push to prosecute so many illegal immigrants. Currently just below 15,000 people are in federal prison for criminal convictions of violations of federal immigration laws. Federal Marshals hold almost another 15,000 immigrants in pretrial. Immigration and Customs Enforcement (ICE) civilly detain another 35,000 immigrants with that number steadily climbing under every administration. These immigrants are housed in federally, or privately run immigration detention facilities, or in local jails under contract with ICE. It's not just immigrants that are coming across the border that we detain. Many people don't know this (Trump voice), but we actually go to other countries, and kidnap individuals suspected of drug offenses, and bring them to the U.S. and incarcerate them. The court system moves at the speed of a slow moving snail so what happens to these individuals is they sit in jail, and wait. Once these kidnapped foreign citizens have sat in jail for a year or two our government offers them a plea bargain of maybe 5 years. So this person then has a choice; do I go to what is probably going to be a fake trial, where I stand no chance of winning, and if I'm convicted I might go to prison for 20 years; or do I take the plea bargain for maybe something I didn't even do, but I can go home in a few years? The immigrants take what is seen as their only option, and plead guilty. The U.S. government prefers not to grant bail. If an individual is sitting in prison doing time, it's counting toward their sentence so by the time they would go to trial they may have completed 30% or 40% of the time they are offered if they plead guilty. The United States has more individuals in pre-trial detention than most other countries even have in prison!

Currently the U.S. has nearly 550,000 thousand people waiting to either plead out or go to trial. While the United States only represents just under 5% of the world's population, we embarrassingly represent almost 25% of the world's prison population. The U.S. has the highest prison population rate at 716 per 100,000. China is the only country that even comes close to the U.S. on total prison population at approximately 1,650,000, but because China has a population of 1.4 billion people China doesn't even come close to the U.S. as far as their prison population rate goes. After China, the prison population totals around the world drop significantly. Italy has a prison population under 60,000 while Libya, and Lebanon combine for just over 12,000 prisoners.

Another point that indicates the prison system is in large part a jobs program is the system is set up to work as a revolving door leading individuals right back to prison shortly after they are released. I understand the need for pre-trial parole officers much more than post sentence served parole officers. Once you have served your time, the government should not be able to keep applying pressure, and watching your every move so they can lock you back up. Each year 626,000 individuals are released from prison. The problem is that large portions from the present year, along with those from a combined number of years where individuals are still on parole, end up going in and out of prison 10.6 million times per year. That statistic comes from various ways people enter, and exit the prison doors. Some people, like myself, made bail, then another charge was brought by the prosecutor so they rearrested me, then the FBI agent, and the state trooper scooped me up for a third time in hopes the judge would revoke my bail. However, the judge let me stay out on house arrest. Myself, and others have to understand if I were black I more than likely would not have made bail at this point. First off, my parents, two of my sisters, and myself all put up our houses for bail. The bail amount was over a quarter million dollars in equity from the homes we had. How many people have access to that? In "Following the Money of Mass Incarceration" Peter Wagner, and Bernadette Rabuy give some fantastic insights on where some of our money is spent, and who benefits from keeping things just as they are. The authors write "Almost half the money spent on running the correctional system goes to paying staff. This group is an influential lobby that sometimes prevents reforms, and whose influence is often protected even when prison populations drop." I remember a shirt that one of the ignorant, Trump-type of correctional officers wore while I was in prison: The shirt was a play on the movie "Field of Dreams" starring Kevin Costner, but it was a portrait of a prison and it stated "build it, and they will come." What an asshole, not Kevin Costner, he's awesome, I'm a big fan; The corrections officer, he's the asshole. Yet, he thinks the prisoners are the pieces of garbage.

Wrongful convictions are a consistent problem in the criminal justice system. Often when an individual is wrongfully convicted, prosecutors and judges do everything they can not to admit they made a mistake. Furthermore, prosecutors usually fight the release of the person who was wrongfully convicted. What kind of immoral, cold hearted animal could take a person's freedom from them for years upon years, find out they did not commit the crime - yet not feel the need to get them out of prison ASAP!? What these immoral prosecutors often do is offer the wrongfully convicted individual an Alford plea. Take the case of James Owen and James Thompson, two individuals that were wrongly convicted of a 1987 rape, and murder. In 2006 DNA evidence from Semen found inside the victim proved the state indeed had the wrong men. Prosecutors, never willing to admit they were wrong, still said they had the right guys, and we're not going to just let these two men out of prison where they were serving life sentences. The unwillingness of prosecutors to admit they were wrong, yet the fact that they knew they were wrong led the prosecutors to offer an Alford plea. An Alford plea offers an immediate release from prison with no retrial, and no risk of a new conviction. If the prosecutors honestly believed the men were guilty why would they offer such a deal? The prosecutors knew they were innocent, and it blows my mind how they can even sleep at night knowing they ruined these innocent men's lives. Mr. Thompson had enough, and took the Alford plea. I guess I can understand to an extent. Prison can mentally defeat a person, and the chance to be free again immediately was just too good to turn down for James Thompson. Plus Mr. Thompson was a weak snitch anyway who actually testified against his "friend" James Owen. The reason I chose this sort of complex case where at one point there was a confession, and some evidence actually did suggest that Mr. Owens and/or Mr. Thompson were the right men, because the police left out crucial evidence, and both the police and the prosecutor withheld details that could have led to the acquittal of Mr. Owens. In a way, fuck James Thompson because he's just as bad as the prosecutor. James Owens however would have none of it. I don't know Mr. Owens, but I feel his resolve, probably fueled by anger, and the need to show his family, his friends, his acquaintances, and everyone else what he said all along was always the truth. Mr. Owens had to wait 16 more months while that piece of garbage prosecutor hoped that he would cave in, and finally take that Alford plea. Just writing this makes me so angry because I saw the heart of these prosecutors, and how little they care about anything other than getting the conviction. Well, that degenerate should at minimum have to serve the 16 months he made Mr. Owens wait for no reason. What kind of individual person would do that? Who in their right mind would do something so unscrupulous? Prosecutor Marvin Brave, that's who. I wish what he did was the exception, but it isn't. All too often prosecutors withhold evidence, and in the rare times they get caught they usually offer the Alford plea so they can in part save face, and not admit their mistake. Also, if the defendant accepts the Alford plea then the defendant cannot sue. It's bad enough that people spend years in prison for something they didn't do, but you don't think the wrongly convicted deserve some monetary compensation? We can't give them back their youth so the least we can do is give them some financial freedom.

Since 1980, 147 individuals who were on death row have been exonerated. Can you imagine how many innocent people have been killed? It's not as if once the state is presented with crucial facts to show the innocence of a defendant they help make sure justice is served. The state continually does the complete opposite. The United States was not always a leader in locking people up. In 1970 there were only approximately 200,000 Americans behind bars and it took the U.S. until 1990 to reach one million people behind bars. The prison population started climbing steadily from the 1970s on though. Once we hit our first million in prison, we quickly doubled that number in only ten years' time. I think it's disgusting that we have gotten to this point, and unless we can restart the Bernie revolution, I don't think we could ever have enough politicians with the moral fortitude to turn these insane numbers upside down. The recent election of Alexandria Ocasio-Cortez gives me some hope though, but the longer AOC has been in office the more it looks as though she is becoming absorbed into the system and will soon enough be a part of the problem as well.

Another reason for mass incarceration is that it's a continued form of segregation. African Americans make up 13% of the U.S. population, and 40% of the U.S. prison population with 60% of prisoners being people of color. I'm not a conspiracy theorist, but our government has always backed policies that segregate

African Americans, and being segregated makes finding success much more difficult. Some segregation types of legislative policies enacted by our government include "The National Housing Act of 1934" where the federal government allowed the Home Owners Loan Corporation to create discriminatory security maps where they would highlight minority neighborhoods in red, and then deny loans in these areas. The Federal Housing Administration furthered segregation by subsidizing builders to build entire suburbs where the houses were only sold to white families. The sales of homes excluded African American families on the basis that selling homes to black families would bring down home values. This maintained a system of housing African Americans away from the rest of society. In New York City for example 85% of the subdivisions built in the 1930s and 1940s had FHA restrictions for selling homes to African Americans.

It isn't that Roosevelt and his New Deal didn't try to help African Americans at all, but when these certain types of programs are created under the mindset of keeping black and white people separated from each other; that's what you get. "The Housing Act of 1937" is a great example of this. This act created approximately 160,000 public housing units for the poor where they placed all poor minorities together. I would think back then the Roosevelt administration thought they were doing wonderful things to help black America, but segregating the poor creates a cycle because that is what you see as you're growing up. In 1944, Roosevelt signed the "Servicemen Readjustment Act" or "the GI Bill." This bill gave education, training opportunities, loans for homes, and job finding assistance. Again, African Americans were discriminated against when they attempted to purchase a home in a white neighborhood. Banks usually would not loan to African Americans, and often realtors wouldn't even show homes in white neighborhoods to potential purchasers who were black. Home ownership in our country is really the easiest way to create any kind of wealth/worth. If you live in a home you purchased for 20 years then you will have a good amount of equity. If you're paying rent for the same 20 years you have built up nothing except wealth for the landlord. Furthermore, if you were to die after the same 20 years of paying on a mortgage there would be a home to pass on to a child. Thus that lack of home ownership gave one part of the population some wealth, while another part of the population contributed to the others wealth in the form of rent. Those homes could have been passed down for generations, and when these FHA and GI loans were given out, African Americans could have afforded to buy a home. Nowadays, it's very difficult to purchase one of those homes in a comparable area. The good news is segregation is less today than it ever has been. Today almost 40% percent of African Americans live in the Suburbs. The benefits that come along with a move from a poor inner city to a suburb can't be over exaggerated; There are better schools, better homes, cleaner neighborhoods, less unemployment, more two parent families. If you see these positive things growing up then you expect nothing less for yourself, and your family.

The problem is that 60% of African Americans who are growing up in inner cities are subject to more policing, and if they make one mistake they are funneled into a system that is difficult to get out of. Prisons are built to put people in them, especially people of color. I believe it's much more of a jobs program, but in order to have that jobs program you need inmates, and where are you going to get those inmates from? From the suburbs? No way! Can you imagine if the jails were filled with young white males like they are young black males? I understand many people believe they are committing more crimes, and that's why they are being locked up at a much higher percentage, and it's not as if they are getting arrested for nothing. Okay, but the truth is many of the crimes involve the sale of drugs; blacks and whites sell and use drugs at about the same rate; about 12%. However, African Americans go to prison for those offenses at six times the rate of whites. I've been going back and forth debating myself; with the closing of the civil rights era, and with African Americans having some success in making political gains for themselves, did our government turn to incarceration as a new means to punish, segregate and subjugate African Americans? Or, did our government start with a few changes in policy, witnessed our incarceration rates rise, see the jobs that were being created, and felt this was a beautiful consequence, and one that must be continued. I tend to believe it was the latter. I think jobs were created; African Americans, and Hispanics were removed from the streets, and our government looked at it as a win-win.

With the exception of job creation, the costs of having the highest incarceration rates in the world are tremendously bad from every other point of view. Breaking down some of the financial costs of mass incarceration is sickening. With all levels of government combined we spend over 80 billion dollars a year on corrections. 80 billion dollars! Republicans!! Democrats!! Think how you can spend that money on dropping bombs on people around the globe, supporting corrupt regimes that brutalize their people, allow our corporations to rape their land, or funneling it to our corporations who fund your campaigns. Just like you are currently doing with funneling our tax dollars to our military industrial complex through the war in Ukraine. Wouldn't that be awesome for you to have all that extra money? I understand your dilemma. What will you do with all those prisoners you release to society and all the jobs that would be lost? We could put them to work rebuilding our crumbling infrastructure. I know, not exactly a new idea, but unfortunately one you really haven't taken to heart, and started either. I know markets for labor have demand, and supply curves just as there is a supply, and demand laws concerning the markets of goods. So in the end just get the people out of prison who shouldn't be there in the first place, and then we can go from there. We need more social workers, and drug counselors so maybe we could train people, and put them to work in those fields.

Probation officers should be social workers, helping former prisoners instead of adding stress to their already stressful return to the real world. For me, being on supervised release was a constant stress, and I would have gladly done another year in prison, and come out truly free instead of being under the government's thumb for four more years. The parole officers will show up at your home or your work out of the blue. It's not as if you are doing anything wrong, but who wants a parole officer to show up at their work. Bosses and coworkers do not appreciate a parole officer showing up where they work. A person on supervised release has to ask permission to do anything. When you are on supervised release you can not live a normal life and you already did your time. 76% of people on probation violate their parole, and return to prison within five years. Do you honestly think the system isn't set up that way on purpose? They need that revolving door in, and out of prison. The constant monitoring of individuals on paper, and the payment of fines helps keep those prison doors open, and makes it near impossible to get yourself out of that cycle of poverty and prison, prison and poverty. When a city levies fines, and the individual is unable to pay then it will usually lead to an arrest. Some cities offer community service for people who can't afford to pay their fines, but many do not. Some defendants are unable to pay a fine because they are homeless or have mental health issues, and the courts rarely ask the defendant why he or she cannot pay their fine. Why would they? Judges understand how the system works, and the poor are the easiest victims. The poor also have the least means to defend themselves. If you are poor, you're going to feel as if this cycle will never end, and you will never get out.

Justice is only for the rich. A great example of this is an unethical, horrible human being, named Dr. James Corasanti. This dirt bag was drunk, texting his then mistress when he hit and killed 18 year old Alix Rice. The impact of Corasanti's BMW snapped the bones of both Rice's lower legs, broke ribs, lacerated her cerebellum, and caused neck injuries among other injuries which resulted in her painful death. Corasanti knew he hit her, and being a doctor certainly could have provided some care and then called an ambulance and possibly saved the young Alix's life. Alix Rice's body was hit so hard she flew 167 feet! A witness heard Rice getting hit because the sound was so loud. Film footage from near Corasanti's home shows Corasanti rushing out of his house almost 30 minutes after the accident. Where to? His attorneys. Corasanti's wife was with him. Neither Dr. Corasanti nor his wife called 911 after parking the car in their garage and seeing the extensive damage, along with the blood and tissue. Somehow the jury acquitted the good doctor. I really don't understand. It's so sad for that poor girl's family and now Dr. Corasanti gets to live his life as if nothing ever happened. If Dr. Corasanti was a poor African American, a poor Hispanic, oh hell, any poor person, they would have been convicted without a doubt. Justice is only for the rich. The rich are getting richer in many ways, but also by way of the prison industrial complex. The crime-control industry in general is a huge money maker and as usual on the backs of the poor. Prisons, and crime prevention industries are publicly funded. It's the construction industry, the real estate industry, the technology industry, the pharmaceutical industry. Plus prisons produce a massive slave labor force.

Companies such as McDonald's purchase goods produced in jails such as plastic cutlery, containers, and have uniforms sewn in prisons. Walmart uses prison labor to strip UPC barcodes and serial numbers from Walmart products so they can be re-sold to after-market retailers. Victoria's Secret isn't what you thought it was; they actually use female inmates in South Carolina to sew undergarments and casual wear. AT&T used inmates to work their call centers! These companies make huge profits, and could pay American workers a decent wage, instead they are increasing their profits by taking advantage of the prison slave labor system. Here are a few other notable companies that benefit from prison slave labor; Bayer, Chevron, Koch Industries, Motorola, Pfizer, Procter & Gamble and Microsoft!

The use of a prison labor force isn't the only way private industries cash in on the prison industrial complex; Companies produce, and sell everything from prison jumpsuits, food trays, mattresses, massive amounts of shitty, expired food, phone services, healthcare, and honestly too many other items to bother listing. All these companies benefit from having large prison populations, and all are extremely happy that America is not the land of the free, but rather the land of lock 'em up. Charging inmates exorbitant rates for making phone calls is criminal in itself. It costs inmates and their families just under $4.00 dollars for a 15 minute call. If the inmate makes a collect call the rates are even worse. Global Tel Link charges an insane rate of $1.13 per minute for collect calls. Most inmates and their family members are not exactly rich, and this puts severe strain on families just to try and stay in touch with their loved one. I'm all for company's making money, but when Global Tel Link is able to make over 500 million dollars annually operating in state and federal prisons, the government should be able to step in and set the rates so everyone benefits. Wouldn't 100 million dollars a year be pretty good? If inmates' families paid .23 cents a minute that would put

Global Tel Link at slightly over 100 million dollars a year. 100 million a year sounds awesome to me, but corporations + politicians = Greed. That equation is the reason prison populations won't decrease. That equation is the reason we are an empire, and need our military industrial complex. That equation is the reason we can't get corruption out of politics. That equation rules our world, and always will, unless we all ban together to say enough is enough.

Conclusion

We need a new massive civil rights movement. We all have to demand political change. We have already seen the solution will not come through the courts, so it has to come through our representatives. "Our" Representatives. I know most of the country believes we have to do something to get our incarceration rates down. I know most of the country believes a defendant should only be sentenced on what he or she either plead guilty to or was found guilty of. So why are we not demanding this take place? Call your state Senator. Demand changes. Call again. Organize protests. Mandatory sentencing statutes have to end, and the larger statute associated with a particular crime needs to be narrowed. This way it leaves judges the ability to adjust sentences, and make sure the sentence fits the crime committed. If we narrow the statutes on the whole we won't see cases where one defendant gets 15 years in Alabama for the same crime a defendant in New York received a one year sentence for.

Any changes in laws need to be made retroactive. We have so many individuals who sold drugs in their early 20s, who are now in their 40s or 50s and are still in prison. The sentences they received were way too long in the first place. Education is the key to prisoners leaving prison better men, and women. I would not want to see free college education for prisoners because I know the backlash would be too great, and I understand. I have $80,000 in student loans so I understand why individuals would be upset if someone in prison is able to get a free education. Just so we are clear, I wouldn't be angry, but I can understand where many would. Therefore we should focus on the trades. Trades are a great fit anyway because they will ensure prisoners are hirable right out of prison.

Parole officers should help prisoners in their return to society. Help give former inmates the tools, and resources they need to make sure they don't return to prison. I'm a huge believer in community policing. We need mentorships with police officers, and inner city youth. We need more police athletic leagues sponsoring boxing, and basketball leagues. I know some fantastic police officers who would be great at leading these types of efforts. Well, not personally, but I've heard they exist. (Just kidding Tony and Scott) (Two family members who are fantastic people, and I'm sure fantastic police officers as well) I often criticize Judges and Prosecutors, but I'm sure one or two of them are fantastic people who are often handcuffed and unable to act in the way they would wish they could or that is just. My friend and fellow Pittsburgh Steeler Fan John Andrews is one of the nicest guys I know and he is an Assistant District Attorney which gives me hope there are many more who are equally kind, caring, good hearted individuals. If you want to get involved tomorrow, start by calling your representative. See what or if the PAL (Police Athletic League) is sponsoring in your community, and work with them on a project that will benefit the community, and maybe that will help change many members of the community's attitudes towards the police.

The following is the letter to Judge Arcara from one of the jurors in my trial:

Dear Judge Arcara,

I am writing this letter in support of James Ventry who was found guilty of witness tampering by the jury of which I served. When I was selected to be a jury member, it was a stressful and scary time for me. I felt unqualified to be making a judgment that could greatly alter the lives of two young men. After listening to almost three weeks of testimony from alleged victims, supposed friends and ex-girlfriends-some of which were perjurers-we as jurors had to make some kind of sense of this information to come to a unanimous decision. Testimonies regarding bookmaking, gambling, home invasions, guns, and "mob" bosses haunted our minds. This subject matter was entirely out of the realm of reality for many of us jurors. To put it simply-we couldn't relate! It was more like a comedy version of the Soprano's. Maybe it's pure ignorance on my part, but how could any of us make a judgment when these people lived entirely different kinds of lives. Well thank God for laws. My very first impression was that these two men probably committed these alleged crimes or this case wouldn't be in federal court to begin with. I thought "Why would the United States waste time and money if they weren't certain they could get a conviction". As testimonies came to an end, I was confused as ever and was looking forward to hearing what the other juror's impressions were. You then spent hours reading us the laws and giving us guidelines to correctly come to a unanimous decision. The words "Beyond a reasonable doubt" hung over all our heads as we returned to the deliberation room. The evidence presented was so dramatically opposed that we all agreed the only believable testimonies came from a Ford dealer, a man who made store signs and the victim of the home invasion. In fact, 11 out of 12 of us had reasonable doubt and we agreed we had to deliver a verdict of "not guilty" due to lack of evidence. For one and half days we tried to reason with one juror who was unreasonable.. We argued collectively that the decisions couldn't be feelings, that we had to go by the guidelines of the law and if her basis for conviction was based on "A gut feeling" that in fact was not evidence but doubt! With the Thanksgiving holiday days away, angry employers becoming less patient, temperatures "heating up" in the deliberating room and mostly, the embarrassment of causing a mistrial, we compromised with one juror to acquit the men on the first four charges and convict Mr. Ventry on the last one. After the verdict was read and each of us stood before you and the court to verify our own verdicts, I couldn't help but feel sad and guilty that I compromised my own beliefs by "cutting a deal" with a person who was just plain ignorant.

After the trial was over and I was able to discuss the case, I found out that a lot of people I know knew of the case and some worked in the same school district as Mr. Ventry. They told me how much he is loved and respected by students, parent, faculty, and the school board. Here is a guy who loves to teach and is an effective teacher. Mr. Ventry is clearly an asset to our society and has worked very hard to accomplish the goals needed to become a positive role model for our children. The fact that he is making a difference right now is what counts. Great teachers are few and far between, I would be grateful to have him teach my own children and make a difference in their lives, especially in the uncertain society we live in now. I am asking you to please overturn the witness tampering charge Mr. Ventry's January 27, 2003 sentencing and get this young man back in the classroom where he belongs!

Respectfully yours,

Name Removed for privacy purposes

Chapter 3-

Military Industrial Complex, and American Imperialism

Much like the prison industrial complex, the military industrial complex is another immoral jobs program, and even more of a money making machine for corporations. Currently we are witnessing a massive transfer of public funds to private corporations for the war in Ukraine. Our military industrial complex is loving what is going on in this proxy war and as always our politicians have no desire to see this war end any time soon. It's another war in a long line of long wars where profits are made at the expense of human lives. We have spent billions of dollars giving military equipment to Ukraine, yet there is no money for anything we need right here in the U.S. We have given Ukraine tanks, helicopters, guns, rifles, helmets, ammunition, and missiles just to name a few military products that we spend our tax dollars on so that our companies can make huge profits. By the end of 2022 we had spent approximately $20 billion dollars arming Ukraine. and currently we are close to having spent an astounding $40 billion dollars. Raytheon Technologies, Lockheed Martin, Noththrop Grumman and Boeing have all benefited big time from the war in Ukraine.

The United States has been in a war time economy since the end of World War II. For the U.S., WWII was the best thing that ever happened for its economy and power throughout the world. The valuable lesson we learned is that producing military goods was good for our corporations, and good for our country. Our leaders began following an endless policy of military engagement throughout the world using the threat of communism as its justification. After WWII, Military spending slowed down for a couple years, but then with the start of the Korean War in 1950 military spending increased to approximately 15% of our GDP. The U.S. has remained war ready or at war, so our spending on our armed forces has always been high, but as far as it relates to our GDP it has fluctuated throughout the years. The cost of U.S. Military spending during the entire Cold War era (1947-1991) was 13.1 trillion dollars, with an average of almost 300 billion dollars annually. 13.1 trillion is an almost incomprehensible number for most of us, but it actually pales in comparison to spending under the War on Terror considering the Cold War era spending took place over almost five decades.

Cold War spending also includes The Korean War, and the Vietnam War. The Cold War victory left our government in search of another reason to keep our military spending at such high levels. The War on Terror is a perfect fit because it can use fear to fight an enemy that can be both real and imagined. The Center for Strategic & International Studies estimates the Afghanistan and Iraq wars are more than five times more costly than the Korean War, and 2.5 times more expensive than the Vietnam War. The Congressional Research Service (CRS) puts the total cost of the Afghanistan and Iraq wars at 1.6 trillion, but that fails to take into account future costs such as medical care for injured military personnel. There have been many studies into the true costs for those wars with most putting the costs somewhere between 4 and 6 trillion dollars. According to the Watson Institute International & Public Affairs, the costs of post September 11, 2001 Wars, Veterans Care, and Homeland Security total 5.6 trillion dollars. The real issue is our politicians have no desire to curtail our military spending in any way. Cutting military spending is a difficult political move for multiple reasons. First off, almost no one wants to propose cuts to our military, and appear to make our country weaker or at least open themselves up to criticism from someone from the opposite political party. Second, just like the criminal justice system, the military industrial complex is a jobs program on many fronts; both home and abroad.

Our top military contractors employ thousands of individuals, make huge sums of money, depend upon global U.S. intervention, and contribute to political campaigns to ensure all remains as is. The top five defense contractors in the United States are Lockheed Martin, The Boeing Company, Raytheon Company, General Dynamics Corporation, and the Northrop Grumman Corporation. There are many others who also make billions including General Electric who earns approximately 3.5 billion dollars a year. That's probably a little more than they earn selling stoves and refrigerators. The war in Ukraine has been extremely profitable for our military contractors. Our military contractors are so tied to Ukraine currently that Northrop Grumman, Raytheon, Pratt & Whitney, and Lockheed Martin were event sponsors at a Ukraine Embassy reception in honor of the 31st anniversary of the country's armed services. Their corporate logos were even on the invitations which show's how they don't even have to hide how much they are profiting. In 2021 our military contractors sold approximately 50 billion dollars in U.S. weapons! War and conflict are good for business and the war in Ukraine has been outstanding. The U.S. has already committed 25 billion dollars to the war in Ukraine with much more to follow. Not only have our corporations profited from the sales of weapons, but because investors understand our government never allows a war to end quickly the military weapon suppliers have also benefited from a rise in their stock prices while the rest of the markets stocks have suffered tremendously. Lockheed Martin employees 126,000 people, and is headquartered in Fort Worth, Texas. Lockheed Martin Aeronautics is based in Marietta, Georgia, and Palmdale, California. Lockheed Martin, like other defense contractors, do not want to see any spending cuts that might diminish their profits. Also, when cuts are proposed, these companies threaten to lay off hundreds of their employees. Yet year after year these companies make record profits. In April 2018, Lockheed Martin reported their first quarter 2018 net sales which were 11.6 billion dollars. In the third quarter of 2022 Lockheed Martin reported sales of 16.6 billion and I'm sure this upward trend will continue as long as the war in Ukraine lingers. Don't worry defense contractors, if somehow the war in Ukraine ends another war is right around the corner. In the rare times as a country when we do scale back spending and these companies threaten to lay off American workers it's more than greedy, it's treasonous. Why aren't these companies who make billions off of our tax dollars expected to show loyalty to those who make them wealthy? Even if there were military budget cuts that lowered defense contractors profits, don't they owe it to their workers to keep them employed? I think that goes for all corporations. If they are losing money, that's one thing, but to maximize shareholder profits at the expense of their employees is inexcusable.

The top 8 defense contractors employ almost 900,000 people, and those contractors use the threat of layoffs every time any cuts to defense spending are proposed. In 2021 Lockheed Martin spent over 14 million dollars lobbying, but don't worry, lobbying pays handsome returns. In that same year, Lockheed Martin generated 67.04 billion dollars leaving them with 6.32 billion dollars in profit. I think when we see these huge numbers the sums almost lose their meaning. So, to put it in perspective, if you have a pretty decent job, and after taxes you clear $800.00 a week, it would only take you about **four million, seven hundred and fifty thousand weeks** to equal the net earnings Lockheed Martin achieved in 2021. You may want to pack lunch. All big companies are spending big money making sure their voices are heard, and their money is well spent. Northrop Grumman spent

12 million lobbying while Boeing spent 17 million lobbying. Boeing's lobbying paid off nicely in 2016 receiving 148 government subsidies totaling over 13 billion dollars. Yet today I saw a meme about limiting what foods someone can buy with their food stamps.

It's crazy how we never seem to care about corporate welfare, but when it's grandma or a single mother, fuck them. The obvious jobs program is the soldiers themselves. According to the Department of Defense, as of January 31st 2018, 1.4 million individuals were serving in the United States armed forces. In Germany we still have 35,000 active-duty troops stationed there. I know we didn't find Hitler's body but come on, I promise he's not coming back. In Japan, the United States has slightly more troops than in Germany with the total being just under 40,000, followed by South Korea at almost 24,000. Combined the U.S. has just under 200,000 troops in a total of 177 countries. If you're unaware or even if you somewhat know, your mind should be blown away by this fact. We have right around 800 military bases in 177 countries. Our government has no desire to eliminate these military jobs, and bring many unskilled workers back to U.S. soil where they would be looking for menial work. Also, the U.S. needs our troops spread across the globe. Why? In part, as previously mentioned, it's a jobs program, and the other reason the U.S. has a global empire is to ensure our corporations protection, their rights to steal other countries natural resources, and sell their goods and services. I'm not saying all the benefits we receive are a bad thing. We have a great, mutually beneficial relationship with the European Union which is our largest trade partner. We limit Russian influence, and share intelligence. NATO would, and does help to defend the United States if or when it were attacked. European allies also cover 34% of the U.S. basing costs, which totals 2.5 billion dollars annually. In Northeast Asia, the United States looks to counter Chinese influence, and support South Korea, and Japan. Our relationship seems to change daily with North Korea due to the erratic leadership of both North Korea's President Kim Jong-Un, and the United States wannabe Dictator, Donald Trump. President Trump did open the door to diplomacy though and I am always in favor of that strategy. So far Biden has also been open to patience and diplomacy and U.S. officials have stated we would meet North Korea anytime and anywhere without preconditions. I think on our end I can't ask for much more, but on North Korea's end with Kim Jong Un in leadership who knows what will happen. In Southeast Asia, the U.S. military protects our trade interests in the South China Sea, which totals about 1.2 trillion dollars in trade with the United States. Due to American oil dependency, U.S. military presence in the Middle East is extremely beneficial to the United States.

Our constant presence in the Middle East is both a good and bad thing. Our presence creates more terrorists, but it keeps the fight against terrorism off of American soil for the most part. I think an at home consequence of increased U.S. fighting in the Middle East is an increase in home grown terrorists. Many individuals who are sympathetic to certain Middle Eastern countries see America's role in the Middle East as an anti-Muslim role. I guess keeping the fight against terrorism in the Middle East is a good thing for the most part though, at least for America. The United States drops bombs, creates poverty, death, and devastation. The question of "why do they hate us" has been asked and answered a million times. We know why they hate us. You can debate on whether their responses to our acts of violence are rational or irrational, but our government understands there is going to be a response. We need a response, otherwise we can't keep dropping bombs, and then we would need a 1980s type Cold War again in order to keep giving money to Boeing, and the likes. Although, I guess when you spend the money these corporations spend lobbying, you don't have to have much of a justification. In 1983, Ronald Reagan came up with the Star Wars initiative (not to be confused with the Star Wars movies). The Strategic Defense Initiative System was a defense against an intercontinental ballistic missile attack. Now, 35 years later President Trump is taking that to another level with creating the sixth independent branch of the U. S. military known as "Space Force". Oh, Trump supporters love the Space Force. One illiterate Trump supporter expressed the reason he liked the idea of Space Force, "because it sounds fucking cool man." Oh Lord, please help us. Our Military already spends about 15 billion per year on space defense items such as, supporting and maintaining satellites for GPS, missile warning and nuclear command and control, but I'm sure the Donald has much cooler things in mind. Perhaps I'm being too hard on the Donald here and Space Force to spite it's cool, but kind of ridiculous name since Space Force is really just taking over roles other military branches previously would have covered. The idea of creating a branch of the military to secure American dominance in space has been talked about for years, but hey former President Trump did make it happen. (Not saying that's a good or bad thing) Since 1983, over 55 billion dollars has been spent protecting the U.S. against missiles launched by the then Soviets, and now the worry is Iran, and North Korea could launch an attack. Oh, and I think Trump mentioned those sneaky Canadians as well. I love Canada by the way. I spent years there boxing at the Shamrock Boxing Club. Some of the best guys, and fighters I've ever met came out of the gym. Okay, sorry, back on point. The truth is the "War on Terror" keeps the excuse for a Military Industrial Complex to keep thriving, and if somehow the war of terror ended like the Cold War did something else would be created to take its place.

Beyond our military, we are in the business of covert operations, involving un-American acts such as overthrowing democratically elected leaders, invasions, and assassinations. The Central Intelligence Agency (CIA) and the National Security Agency (NSA) do the U.S.'s dirty work in these areas. A lesser known agency, the Defense Intelligence Agency (DIA) works to collect, and analyze data. They may be of service at times to the CIA, and the NSA, but in general they seem more defensive than offensive. If Donald Trump colluded with Russia then there would be a big problem, but there doesn't seem to be any actual evidence for this accusation and as far as what Russia did - people from the left need to get a grip. Russia did exactly what they are supposed to be trying to do. Are we up in arms because they were successful? We go so far beyond what Russia did that it's disgusting for people here to act so appalled. The NSA spies both at home and abroad. The NSA also creates computer viruses to cause dismay to our enemy's computer systems. In 2013, Edward Snowden revealed that the NSA was also spying on American citizens, and not just foreign countries. The first bombshell showed Verizon had been providing its customers phone records to the NSA. The NSA, as we would all expect, spies on leaders of other countries. I'm not sure why this was such a shock, other than perhaps some of the taps may have been to the leaders personal phones. Snowden's leaks revealed a number of other insights into what the NSA is secretly doing, including intercepting some 200 million text messages (but shame on Russia for their fake news stories). Honestly, it's "shame on President Obama for not pardoning Mr. Snowden", and for his administration's crackdown, and punishment of fellow whistleblowers.

No other country interferes in other countries' politics more than the United States of America. The United States has such a long history of meddling in other countries' elections, you could say it's in our DNA. This was actually confirmed in a recent Ancestry.com investigation. Okay, maybe not, but Carnegie

Mellon University's Dov Levin found the U.S. interfered in elections over 80 times! Some countries where the U.S. interfered are Guatemala, Brazil, El Salvador, Haiti, Panama, Israel, Lebanon, Iran, Greece, Italy, Malta, Slovakia, Romania, Bulgaria, Albania, Sri Lanka, Philippines, South Vietnam, and Japan. Countries like Iraq aren't included in this list, perhaps an illegal invasion of a foreign country is in a whole other category. The first attempt, and success the CIA experienced in election tampering came in 1948 when it gave funds and support to the Christian Democrats in Italy to beat the pro-Russian Socialist Democrats. I guess that first taste was like when Chris Rock's character "Pookie" got his first taste of crack cocaine in New Jack City. Hopefully Pookie got better because the U.S. is still a raging addict. Again, it's the brainwashing that we have gone through that makes us believe it's okay for the United States to be involved in regime change, but no other country has the right. Almost every U.S. President since Roosevelt has been involved in successful or unsuccessful regime change attempts. When the U.S. overthrows a democratically elected leader it should bother us all. The U.S. loves democracy, no?? I hate the hypocrisy of America.

I don't think it's necessary to cover each immoral act, but a few are worth writing about, and one that I've read quite a bit about, and I found disturbing because of the brutal results was the overthrow and murder of freedom fighter Patrice Lumumba in the Congo. Lumumba was the first Prime Minister of the Congo, formerly the Belgian Congo. Lumumba first turned to the U.S. and the United Nations in hopes of having a smooth transition, and quelling those who were violently fighting for power. The problem was Lumumba was a leader who wanted to use his nation's resources for the betterment of his people, and not the foreign corporations of Belgium, and the United States. Ultimately, Lumumba turned to the Soviet Union, and whether democratically elected or not, that was the final nail in his coffin. President Eisenhower floated the idea to the CIA of poisoning Lumumba, but in the end the CIA supplied weapons and funds to his enemies who eventually murdered Lumumba by firing squad. Sadly for the Congo, the new leader who emerged was the U.S. backed brutal dictatorship of Joseph-Desire Mobutu. Mobutu later changed his name to Mobutu Sese Seko Kuku Ngbendu Wa Za Banga. Oddly enough, I was going to change my name to that until I found out that was Mobutu's full name. Bastard! Mobutu not only murdered his political opponents, he kept his countrymen in utter poverty and despair while paying himself handsomely. Mobutu resided in some amazing properties including a French Riviera Villa, a 15 acre beach resort, an enormous vineyard in Portugal, a huge mansion in Switzerland; and whose property portfolio is complete without a 16th century castle in Spain? It's sad the U.S. would choose to support a man so short sighted, greedy, and brutal instead of a former postal worker who wanted to improve the lives of his fellow countrymen and women. In the end the United States doesn't care how brutal a leader is. As President Franklin Delano Roosevelt said about Nicaraguan leader Anastasio Somoza "Somoza may be a son of a bitch, but he's our son of a bitch". Somoza was friendly to Wall Street, and in the end, what the U.S. fights for is our corporate greed.

Another well-known debacle that shows the United States immoral hypocrisy is the Iran-Contra scandal. They should make a movie about this. Oh wait, they did, a few actually, including "American Made" starring Tom Cruise, and "Kill the Messenger" starring Jeremy Renner. (Loved him in "The Town"). This is a well-known scandal where the Reagan Administration funneled millions of dollars to the brutal Contras through the illegal sale of weapons to Iran. The Contras murdered, raped, pillaged, and then with the CIA's help, trafficked cocaine. Gary Webb first reported the CIA's involvement, and knowledge of the Contra's shipping cocaine into the U.S. in his 1996 series for the San Jose Mercury News called the Dark Alliance. The Contras were flooding South-Central Los Angeles with cocaine, which was then turned into crack, helping create the crack epidemic of the 1980s. According to Contra leader Oscar Danilo Blandon the CIA felt the ends justifies the means. Panamanian dictator Manual Noriega also helped bring arms to the Contras, and was allowed to traffic drugs using the same planes. Noriega, who was actually on the CIA's payroll as early as the 1960s, was often paid over $100,000 a year even though the CIA was well aware of General Noriega's drug trafficking.

It's strange to me how our government partakes in some of the most immoral acts one could think of, yet we still act as if we own the moral high ground compared to other countries. Gary Webb, who initially broke the story, was found dead of an apparent suicide. Mr. Webb shot himself twice in the head. I'm not saying the CIA helped him pull the trigger because there have been cases where individuals have shot themselves in the head twice while committing suicide, but it sure wouldn't surprise me if they did. It should be noted that 99.9% of all individuals who shot themselves in the head twice were either working with our government, mob informants, or had dirt on Hillary Clinton. (99.9% may be a slightly or almost completely made up percentage….. "may be").

The last U.S. sponsored coup I will write briefly about is the 1953 U.S. and United Kingdom backed overthrow of Iranian leader Mohammad Mosaddegh. The democratically elected Mosaddegh led a movement to nationalize the country's oil industry which had been dominated by Britain through the Anglo-Iranian Oil Company. Once Mosaddegh gave the Brits the Iranian boot the British turned to the U.S. who led the coup which placed the Shah back in power until the 1979 Iranian Revolution.

Awe, just seeing the word revolution makes my heart smile. By all accounts Mosaddegh was popular among the Iranian people and what bothers me is he was democratically elected and the U.S. always loves to claim how we are all about democracy until another country elects someone who has the audacity to want control of their natural resources. So instead of having a nationalist as their prime minister, Iranians returned to the monarchy which ruled with the help of the Savak secret police. The United States doesn't care about Democracy. The United States doesn't care about human rights either. The U.S. will always choose a leader that is economically friendly towards us over one that is friendly towards their own citizens. Now we have neither. The Iranians are stuck living in an Islamic Republic that offers little freedom of expression or choice. The 1967 Family Protection Act which provided rights to women in marriage was declared void. Opposition were either jailed or murdered and of course the Shah also murdered many as the monarchy was attempting to hold on to power. Now with Ayatollah Khomeini in power it was mosque based revolutionary bands known as "komitehs" who patrolled the streets enforcing Islamic codes of dress and behavior and issuing whatever punishment they deemed appropriate to any perceived enemies. So both the Shah and Khomeini ruled with violence and brutality. The only one who may have not ruled the way was of course the democratically elected Mosaddegh. It's a shame for both the Iranian people and the U.S. that our government refused to live with the results of other countries' elections. And all of that death and destruction was brought to you by the hypocrisy of the United States of America.

I could go on nearly forever, and give case by case instances of corrupt acts that our government has been a part of that are the opposite of American ideals, but I don't think at this point that's a good use of the reader's time. I just want you, the reader, to understand the depths of what our country gets involved with throughout the world, and how hypocritical it is of us to go wagging our finger at every other country like we are so innocent. What I will do is list a few articles and their subject matter so you will get a pretty good idea on why the United States knows no end to its hypocrisy: In his March 8th, 2014 article for salon.com, Nicolas J.S. Davies titles and writes about "35 countries where the U.S. has supported fascists, drug lords and terrorists." Again, the leader can be a son of a bitch, as long as he's our son of a bitch. Another good read is an article in HuffPost by Ryan Grim and Arthur Delaney titled "The U.S. Has Been Meddling in Other Countries Elections for a Century. It Doesn't Feel Good." The information is out there, and it's endless, but for some reason we are not too bothered by our own immoral behavior.

Former CIA agent and writer Melissa Boyle Mahle stated in her 2008 documentary "Secrecy;" "Should we, as Americans, be involved in kidnapping foreign people, and making them disappear?" "I would argue that's exactly the kind of thing we should be doing." I wasn't expecting Mrs. Mahle to say that, even if she was thinking it. That's the arrogant U.S. way of thinking whether it's the war on drugs or the war on terror. The United States somehow feels it's okay to kidnap citizens of other countries; and those kidnapped, especially when it's within the war on terror realm, often do not have many or any due process rights. 124 States are members of the International Criminal Court, but of course the United States is not. Noam Chomsky said it best in an interview by David Barsamian for the Monthly Review; Chomsky, in speaking about U.S. terrorist acts abroad, sums up my belief on why our international policies continue to create more anti U.S. terrorists. In referring to various U.S. acts that are terroristic, Chomsky states "They are known by the victims, of course, but the perpetrators prefer to look elsewhere." It really is that brainwashing that takes place in us all as we grow up and are taught our history. It's like Winston Churchill said "history is written by the winners". Are we just too lazy to go beyond what our government tells us? Do most of us just really not care enough if it's not happening in our own backyard? It's happening in countries most of us have no desire to visit. We go about our daily lives, and there is no room for the rage in us that we should have for what our government does around the world. Make no mistake about it, if you lived there, if that were your brother, your son, or your sister who was killed by a U.S. bomb or bullet you would find room for the rage.

The U.S. government consistently lies to us citizens in order for us to get behind a war effort. It's been done multiple times throughout our history, and I think what the average person thinks is that was something that happened back then, not now. Of course that's not true, our government always has, and always will lie to us in order to lead us in the direction they want us to go. Everyone is familiar with the lies the Bush administration told us to invade Iraq but in the end, we accept that the administration lied and move on. In his August 26th 2002 speech, Dick Cheney stated "there is no doubt that Saddam Hussein now has weapons of mass destruction and is preparing to use them against our friends, against allies, and against us. Saddam also had biological and chemical weapons and has resumed his efforts to acquire nuclear weapons." On September 7th, 2002, then President Bush referred to an International Atomic Energy Agency report indicating that Saddam was "Six months away from developing a nuclear weapon." Too bad that fucker just made that garbage up. Apparently, the Bush/Cheney speechwriters thought their speeches could be fictitious.

I think all of us left-leaning individuals all expected and figured Bush and Cheney were lying, but when it came from Colin Powell I was thrown a little. Powell didn't come right out and support Bush's desire to invade Iraq, and seemed to be reviewing intelligence reports, and holding out on pressure from the White House to lie. In the end Powell gave in, and betrayed himself and his country when he told lies to the media, and in front of the United Nations. Lies, lies, and more lies. Yet, no one had any real consequences for their lies. Well, I mean no one who participated in spreading the lies. U.S. troops felt the consequences. Iraqi civilians certainly felt, and still feel the consequences. Of course it's always the poor in our country, and throughout the world who pay the price for the lies that lead us to war. From 2004 to 2009, more than 100,000 Iraqi civilians were killed. According to WikiLeaks reports, the vast majority of those civilian deaths were at the hands of fellow Iraqis, but the deaths still stem from our illegal invasion. I think even that fact doesn't resonate at home like it should. Think about it; We, the United States of America, almost as pure of a country as a country can be, invaded another country for completely made up reasons. If any other country did this, we would be drawing up a U.N. resolution condemning the invasion, and probably eagerly preparing for our corporations to make millions of dollars selling weapons while we draw up plans to put our own troops in harm's way.

Our wars always leave behind unbelievable amounts of devastation for decades to come for both the countries we fight, and our own troops. The Vietnam War, and the secret bombing of Laos and Cambodia are great examples of how evil we can be as a country. The truth isn't really taught in American history books. Everything from making Christopher Columbus out to be some kind of hero, and a gentleman, to our involvement in the overthrow of democratically elected leaders around the world. Lastly, to our government's lies, which get us into war, and how we conduct our wars.

I think the lies the Nixon administration told are well documented, and I don't see the need to rehash those. Even though the subject I will speak about is also well documented, I think we frame it in a way that makes its use not seem as inhumane. I'm talking about our use of chemical weapons during the Vietnam War. We often speak about other countries' use of chemical weapons and how immoral those countries are, but I never hear about our use of chemical weapons. We were all taught about our use of chemical weapons, but in using the actual name of the chemical, it almost ignores the fact we used chemical weapons. This is especially true when a teacher is teaching the lesson to high school students. If a teacher is talking about the United States military's use of Agent Orange, I don't think most high school students make the connection; that using Agent Orange is using chemical weapons. Agent Orange is a herbicide. It was made to help clear forest cover, but I think we all can step back and know that our military didn't drop millions of gallons of chemicals, and think it's only going to affect the foliage. An herbicide just sounds much nicer though, right? Agent Orange contains the deadly chemical Dioxin which doesn't sound quite as nice. From 1961 to 1971, the United States military, under the program "Operation Ranch Hand," dropped over 20 million gallons over Vietnam, Laos, and Cambodia. It's sounding less nice by the minute isn't it? Although, I have to say "Operation Ranch Hand" sounds fairly kind. "Operation Ranch Hand" sounds like we might be helping farmers. Hmmm, Trump should have called his socialist program of bailing out farmers after his tariffs "Operation Ranch Hand" that would have been nice too!

The United States didn't stop with their use of Dioxin. The U.S. also continued its use of chemical weapons, and chemical warfare with their use of Napalm. Throughout the Vietnam War, the U.S. military dropped more than eight million tons of napalm incendiary bombs. Napalm burns between 1,500 and 22,000 degrees Fahrenheit. Think about that! Holy shit, where is our decency? How do you drop something like that on other human beings? It also blows my mind how those in power always talk about supporting our troops, but what they do is sacrifice our troops, not support them. The number we hear on how many American soldiers who died during the Vietnam War is 58,0000, with another 150,000 wounded. That number is horrible, but doesn't tell the true story of the herbicide, and the hell it unleashed. According to Nicole Fisher's May 28th 2018 article in Forbes magazine, an "estimated 2.8 million U.S. vets who were exposed to the poisonous chemical while serving and later died." It's so sad, and although many people don't care near as much, there were also more than 4 million Vietnamese citizens who were subjected to the Dioxin poison that was Agent Orange. Is that type of devastation the real legacy of the United States? I wish it were not, but at best it's a mixed bag of creating devastation in one regard, and being charitable in another. The charity we give is usually tied to some corporate profit, but that's not the subject here. Decades, and decades after we dropped millions of tons of bombs, Laotians are still being killed, and wounded by bombs that never exploded. To President Obama's credit, in 2016 Obama increased funding to help clear more unexploded bombs in Laos; but why on earth are people still getting killed or injured almost 50 years after we dropped our last bombs in Laos? If you see the images of Laotians missing limbs, especially when it's children, you can't help but feel both sad, and ashamed at the same time.

The Vietnam War was really the first time American citizens completely understood our government couldn't be trusted. The U.S. government led its citizens astray with lies which led us to war. The anti-war movement was powerful, especially among young people who saw friends, and so many other young people go off to war, and die. Our government, and many right wing leaning individuals were disillusioned with the anti-war movement. The Kent State Massacre was a shameful response by our government, and a response that, as a brainwashed

American, we wouldn't even think was possible here. On May 4th 1970, University students were protesting the bombing of Cambodia by the United States Military. Four unarmed college students were shot, and killed by members of the Ohio National Guard. The four students killed were Jeffrey Miller, William Schroeder, Sandra Scheuer, and Allison Krause. The following is a very brief history of the events that took place at Kent State followed by an interview with Laurel Krause, the sister of the 19 year old honor student, Allison Krause:

On May 2nd the National Guard arrived on the Kent state college campus. There were just under 100 National Guardsmen and about 3,000 protestors. The protestors previously clashed with police and Kent mayor Leroy Satrom declared a state of emergency, and closed all local bars. The closing of the bars turned out to be a mistake as it actually led to more protestors showing up instead of being in a bar having a few drinks. Protestors set fire to the ROTC building and clashed with the firefighters who were trying to distinguish the fire. Due to the volatile nature of the protests on May 4th Ohio National Guard General Robert Canterbury ordered protestors to vacate the premises. Protestors refused to leave and began throwing rocks at various National Guardsmen. The Guardsmen were able to move protestors onto a football field, but also found themselves slightly trapped by the football fence and easy targets for some of the students who were throwing rocks. The National Guardsmen eventually moved up a hill, called Blanket Hill, and this is where things went from bad to really bad. Somewhere between 25 and 30 of those National Guard members said to themselves, "shit, we have M-1 rifles, why are we retreating" upon this realization the guardsman began firing shots into the crowd killing four students, and injuring nine more. It was a sad day for America, and brought the anti-war movement to a whole new level. The following is a synopsis of my conversation with Laurel Krause.

On 10-04-2018 I had a brief, but interesting conversation with Laurel Krause, the sister of Allison Krause. You probably don't need the reminder since it was only about a page ago, but Allison Krause was the 19 year old honor student who was shot, and killed by the Ohio State National Guard during the Kent State student protests. Laurel is in her 60s now, but is still clearly affected by the death of her sister Allison. The pain in Laurel's voice was as if Allison had been killed 3 months, or perhaps 3 weeks ago. I have been lucky enough to never know what it's like to lose a sibling so I can only imagine the pain she felt, and is still feeling. Perhaps fighting for what Laurel believes is justice for Allison has been both a blessing and a curse for Laurel. I think fighting daily keeps the pain of losing a loved one right there on the surface. The pain can never be buried in the place where most of us bury ours. Part of Laurel's search for the truth was co-founding "The Kent State Truth Tribunal" with Emily Kunstler. Emily is an award-winning filmmaker and the daughter of civil rights attorney William Kunstler. Not one of the Ohio National Guardsmen was ever prosecuted. Originally, all eight were indicted, but the charges were later dismissed. That in itself had to be heartbreaking for the family members of those killed. We all want justice when we are wronged, and there is no worse personal feeling than feeling utterly powerless. I suppose that is the one thing all of us in the struggle fight for. We want some power over our own lives and in Laurel's case for those who can no longer fight for themselves. For those families of the four killed at Kent State, they received a lousy $15,000 and a Statement of Regret. Evidence examiner Stuart Allen reviewed a tape of the Kent State Massacre and found an 'Order to Shoot'. This 'Order to Shoot' has been something Laurel Krause, and many others have suspected for many years. The Kent State Truth Tribunal is calling for the Attorney General to examine Mr. Allen's findings, and eventually receive an official acknowledgment for the Kent State shootings by the United States government. Laurel Krause also believes the FBI had an individual among the protesters who may have created the sound of a gun firing so the National Guardsman would have justification to return fire. Laurel spoke about COINTELPRO which she believes may have been involved.

According to the encyclopedia Britannica COINTELPRO was an FBI counterintelligence program that ran from 1956 to 1971. The main goal of COINTELPRO was to "discredit and neutralize organizations considered subversive to U.S. political stability." The program often employed tactics that would be considered illegal. The program infiltrated groups such as the U.S. Communist Party, the Socialist Workers Party, the American Indian Movement, Ku Klux Klan, and spent much of their time on the Black Panther Party. It's even been rumored COINTELPRO sent Forest Gump to have a fight at a Black Panther Party. Some of the tactics COINTELPRO utilized were police harassment, surveillance, and anonymous mailings. The anonymous mailing tactic is something Laurel Krause believes was used to intimidate her family. Laurel and her family received a threatening letter that was supposedly from a neighbor, but Laurel and others strongly believe the FBI's COINTELPRO was behind the threatening letter. Laurel will continue her fight for justice for herself, her family, the families of those killed, and mostly for her sister Allison. If you would like to learn more about the Kent State Truth Tribunal you can go to www.truthtribunal.org

An extremely bothersome program that goes against everything America is supposed to stand for was the Bush/Cheney program of Extraordinary Rendition. The movie "Rendition" starring Jake Gyllenhaal and Reese Witherspoon is fantastic, and does a great job at showing the personal suffering that an individual goes through. I can find a great movie about every subject matter here that you should watch. I love movies.

Okay, back to Extraordinary Rendition. The Extraordinary Rendition program didn't start under Bush/Cheney. The program was started in the early 1990s, but it was taken to a whole new level under Bush and Cheney. Extraordinary Rendition involves kidnapping or capturing individuals who are suspected of having some involvement in terrorist organizations. These captured individuals are then sent to countries such as Egypt, Syria, Jordan, Morocco, Saudi Arabia, Yemen, and Uzbekistan to face interrogations that involve torture. Former CIA agent Robert Baer classified the levels of torture used in various countries and in describing the use of torture in Egypt Baer stated "If you want someone to disappear – never to see them again – you send them to Egypt." Guess where the CIA sent most of their kidnapped souls? We've played this game before, and I think you know how it ends........Egypt. Under the Bush/Cheney program it's estimated between 100 and 200 people were kidnapped and tortured, but who knows if we will ever learn the true number. Unfortunately I think most Americans don't care if we torture some suspected, Muslim terrorist. The United Nations General Assembly adopted the Convention Against Torture and Other Cruel, Inhuman or Degrading Treatment or Punishment in 1984. The Convention was approved and entered into force in 1987. The Convention defines torture as "any act by which severe pain or suffering, whether physical or mental, is intentionally inflicted on a person." The pain or suffering must be "inflicted by or at the instigation of or with the consent or acquiescence of a public official or another person acting in an official capacity." Article 3 of the Convention, which the U.S. clearly violated prohibits States from "expell[ing], return[ing] ('refouler') or extradit[ing] a person to another State where there are substantial grounds for believing that he would be in danger of being subjected to torture."

The United States signed the United Nations Convention Against Torture in October of 1994, but apparently the Bush administration thought they either found ways around violating our agreement or decided some forms of torture were not torture by their standards. Or I guess to the Bush administration, changing the name from torture to "enhanced interrogation techniques" was sufficient. Waterboarding is probably the most infamous torture technique that was used, but it certainly wasn't the only one. Let's take a look at some of these All American illegal uses of torture in these CIA enhanced interrogations. After you read each of these, take a few seconds and close your eyes and picture all these things happening to you. Prisoners were often bound in stress positions. **Stress positions** include, but are not limited to having the person sit on the floor with your legs spread, and holding your hands straight up over your head, standing upright with your hands shackled to the ceiling, or having your feet shackled while holding your hands up. It's been reported that individuals would have to stand in their own feces, and urine. **Sleep Deprivation,** people were often kept awake 100 hours straight. Sleep deprivation may not sound all that cruel, but as someone who has often gone days without sleep, I can attest to how horrible it is, and my experience can't even compare to what they went through while being kept awake. **Cold Water Dousing,** where naked individuals who were shackled and handcuffed were doused in extremely cold water. A suspected Afghani militant held in a CIA black site named Gul Rahman died of hypothermia after being doused in cold water. I know, who cares, an Afghan militant, but the key word there is "suspected." **Cramped Confinement,** where people were confined to a box that would restrict their movement. The CIA agent/interrogator had the option to choose a box big enough to stand in where the agent could question the individual for up to 18 hours or 2 hours curled up tightly in a smaller box. **Facial**

Slaps, Beatings, and Threats, beatings upon arrival, hard slaps to the face and back, and threats that their family would be harmed. Although I'm sure they did much more, I saved the best mental image for last for you, rectal feeding and rehydration. **Rectal Feeding and Rehydration**, where basically you puree food and insert it into their rectum. I'm not sure how that works, but I'm pretty sure you wouldn't get any nutrients by putting food in your ass, so please don't try it. I mean, I'm not a doctor, nor do I play one on T.V., but I was in a couple awesome movies including Crimson: The Motion Picture. All by a film production company I'm a part of called White Lion Studios. (Sorry, I had to give us a plug). Whomever came up with rectal feeding, and rehydration was just a sick CIA pervert.

As everyone should, I hate terrorists. If I saw a terrorist burn someone to death, or cut off their head with a knife I would beat them to death with my own hands if I could. If I saw Dzhokhar Tsarnaev or Tamerian Tsarnaev after the Boston bombing, I would love to have killed them myself. The problem here is that many of these people were suspected terrorists who turned out not to be terrorists, and their lives were wrecked. I know this happens in some CIA black site, or in Egypt, so it's out of sight out of mind. Who cares, but as I stated before if those tortured were your brother, husband, or your father, you certainly would care. All these suspected terrorists have sons, daughters, wives, cousins, and friends. After something like this happens, do they then love America or maybe more likely wish death to America? Torturing someone's family member or friend only deepens the resolve and heightens the animosity someone overseas may have about America. We have to be on that moral high ground we pretend to be on. Experts all agree torture does not produce reliable information. If a person is being tortured they will say anything to get you to stop. I think I'm hard as a coffin nail, but start torturing me, and I bet I will turn soft as cotton. They could kick me in the shins, and I will give the torturer some names. Of course the names I give them will be Judge Richard Arcara, and prosecutor Anthony Bruce. Trinity College Dublin professor and author or "Why Torture Doesn't Work" Shane O'Mara argues "torture does not produce reliable information largely because of the severity with which it impairs the ability to think. Extreme pain, cold, sleep deprivation and fear of torture itself all damage memory, mood and cognition. Torture does not persuade people to make a reasoned decision to cooperate, but produces panic, dissociation, unconsciousness and long-term neurological damage. It also produces an intense desire to keep talking to prevent further torture." See, I told you.

Article 4 of The Torture Convention compels State Parties (meaning us) to criminalize acts of torture as well as "attempt[s] to commit torture" and "an act by any person which constitutes complicity or participation in torture." Complicity, that is the key word, and one I think about often with concern to the United States government. Our lawmakers are complicit in our prison industrial complex, our military industrial complex, as well as our act of aggression around the world. We know George Bush, and Dick Cheney are guilty here of war crimes for being complicit in torturing. We also know nothing will ever come from their guilt, and I like George Bush. I couldn't stand George Bush when he was President, but he has this childlike persona about him which makes me want to think he's not that bad of a guy, just maybe not that bright of a guy.

Donald Rumsfeld, George Tenet, Condoleezza Rice, John Aashcroft, Alberto Gonzales, as well as some high ranking military officers are all guilty of war crimes. Why? George Bush admitted he ordered waterboarding. Dick Cheney still doesn't think there's anything wrong with waterboarding, and every one of those fuckers are complicit. Speaking of complicity; The U.S. didn't really like the use of the word "complicity" in the United

Nations Torture Convention, so when the U.S. enacted their own legislation it was sort of bent to our will just in case we may need to find a way to torture someone. The U.S. senate adopted a reservation limiting the United States commitment under the United Nations Torture Convention. The United States Senate issued the following, "That with reference to Article 1, the United States understands that, in order to constitute torture, an act must be specifically intended to inflict severe physical or mental pain or suffering and that mental pain or suffering refers to prolonged mental harm caused by or resulting from: (1) the intentional infliction or threatened infliction of severe physical pain or suffering; (2) the administration or application, or threatened administration or application, of mind altering substances or other procedures calculated to disrupt profoundly the sense of the personality; (3) the threat of imminent death' or (4) the threat that another person will imminently be subject to death, severe physical pain or suffering, or the administration or application of mind altering substances or other procedures calculated to disrupt profoundly the senses or personality. (b) That the United States understands that the definition of torture in Article 1 is intended to apply only to acts directed against persons in the offender's custody or physical control.

This last sentence contained the key that unlocked the door for Attorney General Alberto Gonzales, Vice President Dick Cheney and President George Bush. When Alberto Gonzales read "Article 1 is intended to apply only to acts directed against persons in the offender's custody or physical control" Mr. Gonzales instantly got erect, and said holy bleep!!! George, Dick, Dick, Dick!!! Why the hell did I "bleep?" I've been swearing all over the place, "Holy Fuck!!!" That's what that asshole Alberto said. Although if Mr. Gonzales would have read what the Foreign Affairs Reform and Restructuring Act of 1998 stated, maybe Mr. Gonzales would have changed his "Holy Fuck" reaction to "Awe fuck." I'm pretty sure he was quite aware of what the policy stated, but since you may not be, here it is. "It shall be the policy of the United States not to expel, extradite, or otherwise effect the involuntary return of any person to a country in which there are substantial grounds for believing the person would be in danger of being subjected to torture, regardless of whether the person is physically present in the United States." That's pretty clear Alberto.

As I stated previously the program of Rendition was started in the 1990's and although I'd love to place the whole shameful blame on the Bush Administration, the Clinton Administration did the exact same thing. The Republican Bush administration was worse, but the Democratic administrations of both Bill Clinton, and Barack Obama shouldn't exactly be proud of their behavior in ignoring the United Nations Torture Convention. Under the Clinton administration, individuals were captured by the United States, sent to other countries under the Rendition program, and then executed by the country we sent them too. When Barack Obama ran for President he often criticized the Bush administration for Extraordinary Rendition, but when Mr. Obama became President Obama he suddenly didn't have the same moral fortitude as he did prior to becoming President.

Between continuing Rendition, and immensely increasing drone strikes; when it comes to those types of human rights issues, President Obama was not the change most informed, liberal minded people hoped for. Not that President Obama wasn't a huge improvement from the Bush administration. President Obama closed the CIA's secret black sites and no longer gave the CIA permission to use Bush and Cheney's enhanced interrogation techniques. As you can imagine, President Trump wouldn't have any moral qualms about rendition or torture. Actually, I can't imagine Trump would have any moral qualms about anything. I'm not positive, but I think in order to have a moral qualm, you would have to have morals. Nope, no morals or moral qualms for that man. Trump's pick for Director of the CIA was Gina Haspel. Mrs. Haspel operated former CIA black sites and drafted orders to destroy evidence that would have divulged torture. Trump continually talks tough, and threatens to bring back torture, but he has been highly secretive when it comes to what his administration is actually doing in the fight on terror.

Indefinite detention is horrible, and has shamefully remained in effect to this very day. Even if someone might be a terrorist, I don't see how anyone can think 15 years in prison without being charged or even allowed one day in some type of court could be okay. I get it, these people might be dangerous terrorists, but they might not be. I also understand that when many people hear their names, it doesn't necessarily encourage empathy. The suspected terrorists' names are Mohamed, Feras, or Ayman. If those who were locked up without even being charged were named Jacob, William, and James… maybe a little more outrage would be out there. To be fair, let's give credit where credit is due. First, the President on just his third day in office did order the detention facilities at Guantanamo to be closed no later than one year from the date of his order. President Obama wasn't able to get Guantanamo completely shut down, but President Obama did drastically reduce the prison population in Guantanamo. Currently there are only about 40 detainees remaining at Guantanamo, down from the more than 700 it contained at Guantanamo's height. Either way, 700, 400, or 40; just charge these people and if they are guilty, convict them and give them life in prison. As we all know, there are no shortages of prisons in 'Murica.'

Conclusion

There's just too much money involved so.....we're fucked, and so are the poor countries we continue to crush. Okay, you don't want to hear that bleak forecast. Unfortunately, when it comes to our military needs we have had the same mindset for 80 years now so we aren't going to change that mindset in a few short years. We have to slowly decrease funding to the Pentagon. I don't think anyone can make the argument successfully that we need a military the size of ours to fight the current war on terror. I also don't see any way in which we can reduce our Military size quickly, and reintroduce tons of both skilled and unskilled individuals back into the workforce. I'm sure some people will be offended by the "unskilled" reference, but what I mean is those individuals may have skills that are relevant to life in the Marines, but not so much in the civilian world. We have to reevaluate how many bases are needed, and where those bases are needed. The bases can be slowly closed over a ten year period with plans to reeducate and re-skill those individuals reentering the civilian world.

I mentioned earlier we have approximately 35,000 troops in Germany and just under 40,000 in Japan. Do we need that many in those countries? No, of course not, but maybe we can make everyone happy by keeping those bases open and keeping the troop count high or maybe even higher. Germany and Japan are countries we have great relationships with, and those countries do not see us as unwelcome guests. However, we offend many other countries by having bases in their backyard. When I was a kid, I got into a fight with a neighborhood kid who was in my backyard. If he wasn't in my backyard we probably wouldn't have gotten into a fight. Why the hell are we in everyone's backyard who doesn't even like us? We are uninvited house guests who show up with weapons, set up a spot in the corner of your backyard and never, ever, ever go back home.

Let's close Military bases in countries like Iraq, and Afghanistan. By keeping many of our Military bases open in U.S. friendly countries, we will be able to keep our Military jobs program alive and well. We need to be smarter in how we deploy this jobs program. I would love to see our military get a complete overhaul but the reality is it's not going to happen, so let's try to come together on a solution that everyone can live with. I can accept that bases both home and abroad create jobs, and I'm okay with that, but we can also recognize that the military is a jobs program and make some adjustments to treat our military employees more like regular employees. For starters, how about we up the retirement age? To retire from the military, and receive a military pension, an individual must stay in the military for 20 years or more. Therefore, if an individual retires as an E-8 after 20 years he or she will collect about $22,000 a year. Plus, if the retiree doesn't get their health benefits through a spouse, they can purchase a plan through Tricare at a much lower cost than traditional health insurance plans.

Most everyone is thankful to those who have served or are currently serving, but I think the retirement age could be moved more along with that of the rest of our country which would save our country millions of dollars each year. Finally, an audit of the Pentagon's spending needs to (finally) take place. No one even has a clue as to the millions of dollars lost through waste and corruption. We have auditors who investigate certain aspects of waste of U.S. taxpayer funds but nothing as comprehensive as we need. Although, what these auditors do point out should make us angry enough, but as usual apathy is all we are capable of. Inspector general John Sopko pointed out billions of dollars in wasted funds in Afghanistan. The corruption included weapons disappearing as soon as they arrived, and planes being donated to local government that doesn't need them. Our corporations keep getting paid to produce the planes and weapons. The money is getting spread everywhere one way or another so our politicians are only too happy to pretend they are mad. Our politicians claim they are going to make changes but…... Sopko's report was done in 2012, and since then nothing has changed. The reason nothing changes is because the government continues to do their number one job, which is funneling our tax dollars to corporations. The main point is; if we stop the corruption, and if we spend our money wiser, we can keep an enormously large jobs program, cut down on the new terrorists we create, and spend the money we save on infrastructure and education.

Chapter-4

Democrats and Republicans A One Party System?

"Fascism should more appropriately be called corporatism because it is the merger of state, and corporate power." -Benito Mussolini-

Neither the Republican or Democratic Parties work for us. Both parties are corrupt and work for corporations and the billionaire class. There are a few differences between the parties, and I think there are enough differences where I can say for most of us the Democrats might be about 2% better than the Republicans.. Unfortunately, what the two party system we presently have leaves us with is a corrupt, two party system with one party slightly better for 95% of us, but neither party really cares about you. Even though both parties are horrible it does blow my mind how anyone who is not wealthy can be fooled by all the social issues into voting for the party that is laughing at you behind your back and calling you white trash while they continue to be the real takers.

First off, let's make no mistake about it; Corporations, through their lobbyists, are running this country. I thought, incorrectly, that since big oil often not only does not pay taxes, but they actually have we, the U.S. taxpayers, paying them in the form of subsidies, that they would be the largest contributor to political campaigns. Energy industries rank number 9 in campaign contributions with the evil, influential Koch Industries leading the way and contributing $5,698,840.00 through 2017-2018. Koch controlled organizations spent more than $1.1 billion dollars during the 2020 election cycle. Koch Industries contributions are not to be confused with the Koch brothers and their political networks donations. The Koch brothers laugh at nearly $6 million. With the Supreme Court clearing the way with their Citizens United decision, the Koch brothers and their like-minded friends spent $400 million in a losing effort to stop the reelection of President Obama. The network regrouped in 2013, and bought and paid for many Republican seats in the U.S. Senate, and they saved $100 million in the process. Go Cock brothers! I mean Koch, sorry. Currently the Koch network has raised more than $70 million dollar for new anti-Trump ads to challange Trump in the Republican primaries.

Like most corporations, those in the Energy field spend money on both parties, but the energy industry gives far more to Republicans. The top 5 are Republicans, all receiving about a half million or more with Democrat Heidi Heitkamp from North Dakota coming in at number 6 receiving almost a half million herself. However, 19 of the top 20 energy industry money grabbers are Republicans. The energy sector has over 600 firms and associations lobbying for their interests, so there is plenty of money to go around. However, when it comes to energy interests, especially oil corporations, their money is for the most part given heavily to Republicans.

So, what is the return on Oil and other energy companies lobbying investments? The return comes in various forms often in policies not being enacted. For example; Oil companies such as ExxonMobile, Shell, and various others spend millions of dollars each year opposing climate change policies. The result of not having climate change policies enacted is fantastic for the oil companies, but horrific not just for the rest of the country, but for the rest of the world. Sometimes lobbyists have competing interests. The funny thing is when no one is lobbying for a bill it almost never passes. No money = No bill. I think that was one of

Newton's Laws. Solar is at odds with the Utility companies; including electric, coal, and nuclear. Now, the Utility companies are fighting back, and slowing down the growth of solar power. Solar power in the U.S. has more than tripled since 2012 but the growth rate is slowing in large part because of push back, and the pushing in of money from the Utility companies. Utility companies through lobbying efforts are getting some states to phase out "net metering," where a solar power owner can sell back power to the grid. Utility companies are also getting states to stop giving tax credits to individuals who purchase solar. Hopefully Governor Hochul in New York never does either of these as solar is so important to our future and on a selfish note I just signed a contract to have solar panels installed on my home in Niagara Falls, NY and as of this writing the solar panels have been installed and have been up and running for a couple of years now.

California is truly leading the way when it comes to solar. California will require solar power for all new homes, and California law requires at least 50% of the state's electricity to come from non-carbon producing sources by 2030!!! Yayyyy California! I hope once other states see the success California has with solar they will follow their lead. California is committed to renewable sources of energy and is putting their money where their mouth is, but it's the non-renewable energy sources that unfortunately receive more subsidies. Clearly this isn't driven by what is best for our future. The subsidy amounts are driven by the dollars those industries can pour into campaign contributions and lobbying efforts. The U.S. fossil fuel industry is directly subsidized billions of dollars each year, and according to the International Monetary Fund (IMF) indirectly the oil industry costs taxpayers trillions of dollars. Some of the costs are consumption subsidies, which are a good thing on the whole, but what if instead of subsidizing the consumption of fossil fuels we converted these low income homes to solar?

At least the solar panel companies will be paid off at some point. For example, I am getting solar panels installed to supply electricity to my 3500 sq. ft. home. I had to take out a 12 year loan, at 5% interest, which amounted to approximately $250.00 a month. The $250.00 dollar monthly payment amount is actually less than my current electric bill, and because my home has electric heat the cost will be about 4 times less in the winter months.

Another indirect cost of the fossil fuel industry is the amount of time and money the U.S. military has to spend protecting shipping routes. Protecting oil and its shipping routes is another reason our Military needs such a significant presence in the Middle East. Lastly, the climate costs go far beyond the financial costs, and result in the loss of lives. According to Oil Change International, which is a research organization focused on showing the true costs of the fossil fuel industry; in the 2015-16 election cycle the energy industry, including oil, gas, and coal companies spent over 350 million dollars in campaign contributions, and lobbying efforts. In return for those investments or those contributions, and lobbying efforts they received almost 30 billion dollars in federal subsidies. As usual, campaign contributions, and lobbying efforts are money well spent.

Okay, you get the point on energy industries so let's focus a little on the number one lobbying industry. And the winner is.......The Pharmaceutical Industry! "Oh, thank you so much, we thought for sure the insurance industry, or oil and gas would win, but we are so proud of ourselves for never giving up and recognizing that spending 1 dollar in lobbying will earn us many, many more in sales. First, I'd like to thank the lobbyists, without them we wouldn't be able to bribe congress with our contributions. Well, sure we could, but we'd have to do it ourselves. Second, and most importantly, we want to thank those we bribe (you know who you are) without you we might actually be in the free market system we all pretend to love, and then we might have to sell our drugs for far less money, so thank you, thank you from the bottom of our bank accounts. Lastly, we do want to apologize quickly to those who started out on our pain killers, and who ended up on heroin. It was an unfortunate, unforeseen result that we never, ever, in a million years thought could be possible. Thanks again."

In 2018 the Pharmaceutical industry spent over 150 million dollars in lobbying. The pharmaceutical industry needed to buy influence to get that Covid cash so in 2022 the pharmaceutical industry spent an insane $373.74 million dollars! In 2018 the top spender was the Pharmaceutical Research & Manufacturers of America at almost $16 million with the number two contributor, Pfizer Inc. spending slightly over $6.5 million. Now because of the amount of money being funneled from the taxpayer to the pharmaceutical industry due to Covid lobbying has really ramped up. In the first quarter of 2021 the pharmaceutical industry spent over 92 million dollars setting a quarter record! The Pharmaceutical Research & Manufacturers of America is a trade group representing various companies in the pharmaceutical industry, advocating for public policies that make life easier and more profitable for those they represent. PhRMA represents companies such as 3M Pharmaceuticals, GE Healthcare, Johnson & Johnson, Merck & Co., Inc. and even the number two lobbying spender Pfizer Inc. Trump promised to use his amazing deal making skills to reduce the cost of prescription drugs but after meeting with top industry executives in Trump's first month in office, nothing has been done. Money talks and I'm sure those executives explained their role in contributing to the financial health of the Republican Party. Reportedly, the executives "educated" President Trump. I'm sure they did, they educated him on them being on the same money team as President Trump and things are no different now that Joe Biden, a Democrat, is in office. The Pharmaceutical Research & Manufacturers of America not only lobby, but they advertise, and advocate for the pharmaceutical industry on the whole, and they have done a great job at shifting some of the blame away from the pharmaceutical companies.

While big Pharma is putting the blame elsewhere they are continuing to generate enormous amounts of money. In 2016, Johnson & Johnson generated revenue of 71.89 billion dollars. This increased during the pandemic as in 2020 Johnson & Johnson revenue skyrocketed to 82.58 billion, then in 2021 revenue increased even higher to a whopping 93.77 billion. Maybe Johnson & Johnson should change their name to Johnson **$** Johnson. Percentage wise Moderna saw an even steeper increase in revenue than Johnson & Johnson in those same years. Moderna reported a total revenue of 18.5 billion dollars for 2021 up from a missmal 803 million in 2020. I'd be happy with the lowly 803 million, but by anyone's standards that is one huge increase. Pfizer, (who are well known for their little blue pill), generated revenue of 81.3 billion in 2021, up from 41.7 billion in 2020. Just like the effects of that little blue pill on men, the future of Pharma revenue will continue to rise. Global Pharma is estimated to reach 1.12 trillion dollars in 2022, but because of the covid cash cow big pharma exceeded expectations and raked in 1.4 trillion dollars. Roche was predicted to come in at number one with sales of 52.6 billion, Novartis comes in second with sales of 52.5 billion while Pfizer will round out the top three with sales just under 50 billion. Yet again Covid changed the landscape and because of "vaccine" sales Pfizer rose from the sixth largest revenue generator to claiming the top spot in 2022. Congratulations on getting the government to force millions of Americans to choose between feeding their families or taking a shot they may not have wanted or needed. Don't feel too bad for Roche, the pharmaceutical company still managed to finish the year claiming the number three spot while Johnson $ Johnson finished the year in the number two spot.

Both parties rake in the money from lobbyists and just like Hillary Clinton getting paid to give speeches to Wall Street, you're not giving out money without a pretty much guaranteed return on your investment. Four out of five of the 2018 top recipients from lobbyists are Democrats. The top five are;
1. Sherrod Brown (D-Ohio) $517,091.00 2. Jon Tester (D-Montana) $497,213.00 3. Paul Ryan (R-Wisconsin) $453,131.00 4. Heidi Heitkamp (D-North Dakota) $444,666.00 5. Claire McCaskill (D-Missouri) $380,971.00

There's another sneaky way in which former Members of congress can use their connections and influence to earn themselves and their lobbying firms money. Former Speaker of the House Newt Gingrich, and former Senate Majority Leader Tom Daschle (who both sort of just fit that "sneaky" definition to a tee) work for lobbying firms, but never register as a lobbyist. Instead Gingrich and Daschle call themselves advisors, and are part of a revolving door between government and the corporate world. Gingrich denies being a lobbyist, and insists that his consulting firm "The Gingrich Group" solely provides strategic advice, not lobbying. I doubt there is any difference. Lobbying is by far the most popular and often lucrative career for a former member of Congress. The lobbying boom happened between 1998 and 2004 when almost half of all the 200 House members who left office for one reason or another became a lobbyist. Those leaving Congress at the end of more recent terms still often lobby, but like the aforementioned Newt and Tom, they often do it as "advisors" making a shady, corrupt system even more shady and corrupt.

The reason they call it a revolving door is that it's not just former Congressman becoming lobbyists, but lobbyists who get jobs within the government in Washington. Does anyone actually believe they aren't working out deals with corporations they formerly lobbied for? It's like the saying goes, "when one door shuts, another opens" only this time it's everyone in Washington knowing how the system works, and that they all must play the game, and they all get rewarded. The reward is money for campaigns, bills passed in congress, jobs for corporations you helped pass laws for, and jobs for lobbying firms. It's an endless cycle, and they are all getting filthy rich while we all pay the bill. Those "drain the swamp" policies Trump promised are lost here as well. According to ProPublica Trump had almost 280 political appointees who were all former lobbyists. Geez people, don't let the revolving door hit you in the ass. I'm about to shock you for a brief minute. Ready? Trump actually had those appointees sign a five year prohibition on engaging in lobbying activities with respect to an appointee's former agency and a lifetime ban on engaging in activities on behalf of a foreign government or political party that would trigger registration under the Foreign Agents Registration Act of 1938. Go Trump! Oh wait, damn it, just before Trump left office Trump rescinded his executive order. Of course Trump rescinded the order. President Biden had his appointees sign a similar pledge so let's hope Biden doesn't go back on the Biden Pledge as Trump did on the Trump Pledge.

As I stated earlier; both the Democrats and the Republicans are bought and paid for by corporations, but clearly how much corporations give to the two parties indicates who those parties look out for more, and where their values are (if they had any to begin with). I want to point out some significant differences between the two parties, and why all you middle class, and lower middle class Republican voters are plain fools. Let's start with commercial banks like Wells Fargo, Bank of America, and JP Morgan Chase. In 2014, 72% of the industry's donations went to

Republicans. The remaining 28% went directly to Hillary Clinton. (I'm kidding) Don't you know me at all by now? Looking at the 2017-18 range, the trend appears about the same. For example: of the $2,014,104.00 dollars the American Bankers Association donated, $1,502,903.00 dollars went to Republican candidates. JP Morgan Chase, Bank of America, and Wells Fargo all gave fairly equally to both parties with Republicans only getting slightly more. As you move to donations under a million dollars, the vast majority went to Republican candidates. Citizens First Bank and International Bank of Commerce gave 100% of their donations to Republicans, while SunTrust Banks gave Republicans $361,671.00 of their $431,307.00 dollar total.

On the whole Democrats want some minor consumer protection bills that reign in the banks such as the Dodd-Frank banking reforms. The Republicans rolled back Dodd-Frank with 33 of the 258 votes to pass it through the House coming from the Democrats. The bill eases restrictions on banks, and raises the threshold from 50 billion all the way up to 250 billion where banks are deemed too important to the financial system to fail. Now, those banks would no longer have to have the stress tests that were put into place in order to avoid the exact financial disaster of why Dodd-Frank was enacted in the first place. You know who you think would be really upset about this? Former U.S. representative from Massachusetts Barney Frank. Do you know who isn't upset about the bill? You guessed it, Mr. Barney Frank. If he was still a member of Congress then I believe he would be enraged, but since Mr. Frank is a hypocrite who now works for the banking industry, good old Barney thinks this bill is fantastic, and now says the 50 billion dollar mark was far too low.

The one thing I will say about Republicans, they are not hypocrites. They may fool the white trash dummies with social issues, but they make no bones about wanting all the money. Republicans never blamed the banks or thought the banks needed any regulation in the first place. Trump's 2019 budget proposal calls for 15.3 billion dollars in cuts to Medicare and 6.5 billion dollars in cuts in the first year alone to Medicaid. Republicans have wanted to privatize social security as well. You didn't make enough money in your lifetime to put enough aside to support yourself in retirement…..Fuck you. You can't afford healthcare for yourself or your children…Fuck you. You didn't earn enough to pay for your own health insurance as a senior, or at least take on much more of the cost sharing……Well, Fuck you too, you old, poor bastard!

When it comes to climate change, Democrats seem to at least believe it's happening and understand it's actually a bigger threat to our security than the over-inflated threat of terrorism. Republicans either outright deny it or grudgingly admit to it, and usually add some kind of bullshit that's pro-business, and won't restrict polluting corporations in any way. Many Republicans also believe the good Lord will handle it, thus, this all must be a part of God's plan anyway. President Trump pulled the United States out of the Paris Accord in which 195 state parties have signed the agreement to strengthen the global response to the threat of climate change. In part, Trump pulled out because he got confused and thought he was supposed to do the same thing he did while having sex with Stormy Daniels. Trump is also motivated by his usual desire to undo everything President Obama did. Trump's administration is filled with climate change deniers and even if someone within the administration believes in the negative effects of climate change, I'm certain they understand they need to temper their voice for fear of Trump's wrath. Climate change deniers within Trump's administration include: Trump's Attorney General Jeff "the leprechaun" Sessions, Secretary of Energy, the guy who takes stupid to a whole new level, Rick Perry, Agriculture Secretary Sonny Perdue, Homeland Security Secretary Kristjen Nielsen, Vice President

Mike Pence, and the biggest idiot denier would be President Trump himself who thinks coal is the power source of the future. President Trump once stated "The concept of global warming was created by and for the Chinese in order to make U.S. manufacturing non-competitive."

Trump constantly tweeted about it being cold outside as evidence that global warming is a hoax. Apparently Trump is confused, and doesn't understand the difference between climate change, and the weather. I could understand if he joked about it once or twice when it was super cold, but Trump has referred to global warming or climate change in over 100 tweets. Trump even removed climate change from the Pentagon's National Defense Strategy. Trump's ignorance on almost every subject knows no bounds, and you have to wonder, does his cult now question the existence of global warming? Well, I googled it and according to a 2017 article in the Washington Post only 25% percent of Trump supporters believed climate change is happening now and is caused by humans. I guess that's not exactly surprising. Trump supporters aren't exactly scientists are they? Although, you don't have to be a scientist to believe global warming exists, you just have to believe in science. I don't want to give Hillary Clinton supporters too much credit but 90% of Clinton voters at least believe global warming exists. Clinton voters still fall short of the 100% of Bernie believers who believed in both Bernie, and the fact that climate change is happening. (I made the 100% up, I'm fairly confident it's accurate, but I will allow for a 1% margin of error ☺). Ending on a positive note, the Democrats having some sort of conscience whereas the Republicans have none under President Biden the United States rejoined the Paris Agreement.

Conclusion

Although corporate money is what dictates American policy at home, and around the globe there are a few significant policy differences between the two parties. If you are a multi-millionaire who has social views that line up with the Republican Party, then you should by all means be the asshole you are, and vote Republican. However if you are not wealthy, you have no business voting for Republicans. It goes beyond all levels of stupidity to vote against your own economic interests just because you're against gay marriage. What are the other reasons someone who is not wealthy is voting Republican? Welfare is often a subject that angers middle class Republican voters. I've heard Bernie Sanders make the argument that when a low wage Walmart or McDonald's worker is subsidized by collecting food stamps, we aren't actually subsidizing the worker, but we are subsidizing those companies, and their unwillingness to pay a high enough wage. If companies like Walmart paid a high enough wage then these workers wouldn't need government assistance. It's not as if Walmart can't afford to pay their employees a higher wage, they just refuse to so they can keep more of our money.

I have a brother who lives in Arizona who got hired for a skilled labor job, and they started him out at $12.00 dollars an hour! His kids are older so he doesn't have a family to support any more, but if he did the kids would either starve or they would need some help. My brother isn't someone who would take the help so I'm sure he would get a second job before he took any help, but why should he or anyone else have to, just so corporations can earn more of profit? I was putting a new roof on my house last summer, and afterwards I spoke to the gentleman who drove the truck, and loaded the bundles of shingles onto the conveyor belt for the rooftop delivery. I had given him a tip, and during our conversation the subject of wages came up. I asked him how much he made and he replied $13.00 dollars an hour. I was surprised that he had to drive a huge truck and load heavy bundles of shingles all for $13.00 dollars an hour. When I first heard the proposal of paying McDonald's workers $15.00 dollars an hour I thought it was too high, but as long as it's for full time workers it isn't too high. Plus, like the saying goes "a rising tide lifts all boats." The hope is if McDonald's or Walmart has to pay their full time employees a "livable wage" of $15.00 dollars an hour, how can these other corporations continue to pay low wages for skilled positions? The answer is they can't. These companies will have to pay these men and women a respectable wage. It's not as if there isn't plenty of money to go around. Jeff Bezos, the owner of Amazon, makes more money in 10 seconds than the median Amazon worker makes in a year. I'm not saying the owner shouldn't make the lion's share of the money, but the greed of all these corporations is insane.

We have to demand they spread the wealth around to more of their employees. Not to mention companies like Amazon avoid federal taxes which in the end costs us. According to Mathew Gardner of the Institute on Taxation and Economic Policy Amazon avoided approximately $5.2 billion dollars in federal taxes in 2021. Amazon reported record profits totalling more than 35 billion dollars and paid a tax percentage on those profits of only 6%! That's criminal. We have to tell our representatives this is unacceptable. Other social issues that get the majority of white voters who earn $30,000 to $50,000 dollars a year to vote Republican include immigration, racial tension, gay rights, the abortion issue, and lastly, another issue the Republicans do a fantastic job fooling the fools about is gun rights.

President Trump himself claimed if Democrats win a majority in Congress "they'll take away your 2nd Amendment." The false claim that Democrats want to take away your guns is a belief firmly held by most uneducated, lower income Republican voters. Republicans spread the lies, and fuel the fire, but as usual there's no truth to what they are saying. Democrats are gun owners who often have the same limited understanding of the Second Amendments original intent as Trump voters do. The Second Amendment was ratified in 1791 and states "A well regulated Militia, being necessary to the security of a free State, the right of the people to keep and bear Arms, shall not be infringed." I don't know anyone in a fucking Militia. Do you? Without spending much more time on this; The second amendment was written when you could actually rise up against your tyrannical government, and attempt to overthrow it. Go ahead, get 20,000 of your best buds together, and give it a shot. See how fast our government crushes you. Democrats want some sensible gun laws that almost everyone is in favor of. The Democrats do not want to take your guns, or give theirs up either for that matter.

We need to kick the Republicans out of office and keep them out. Then once they are out we need to start kicking the Democrats out next. This narrative that 3rd Party candidates can't win has to be changed, or we have to change the Democratic Party, and I don't mean just moving it to the left on social issues. Corporations have to stop controlling our country. They are the reason we drop bombs everywhere. They are the reason we have a CIA that does things around the world that make other countries wish we were like Russia and only created bullshit memes. They are the reason we spend more money on healthcare than any other country yet we don't see better health outcomes. This is supposed to be a government of the people, for the people, and by the people. However, what we have is a government of the corporations, for the corporations and by the corporations. We need to kick all these greedy corporations the hell out of our government! I think first, we may have to kick the politicians out though.

Chapter-5

African Americans in America

On my first day of kindergarten I met Tony Blackman, and that day or sometime that week he came over to my house to play. I also met Willie Santiago who I also brought over to my house that week. My dad, who up till the day he died was a workaholic, happened to stop home briefly both days, and met both Tony and Willie. My father could have said, "You can't bring home black and Puerto Rican kids to play with," but he didn't. The only thing I remember my father saying was "they seemed like nice kids." I also remember going to my grandma and grandpa Bellavia's house on Sundays at 1:00 p.m. for macaroni and meatballs. My grandfather being from a different era and generation was very racist. I remember watching basketball or football games, and that's all I would hear out of his mouth was "nigger this," and "nigger that" and I hated it. I couldn't stand going there, and listening to him. When we were on his porch my grandfather would point out houses in the neighborhood where he and my grandmother lived in downtown Niagara Falls, NY, and say "that used to be Italian or Polish, and now a nigger lives there," and etc. etc. Magic Johnson was one of my heroes growing up so when I saw Magic running and smiling, I saw someone I wanted to be, not what my grandfather saw. I emulated Magic Johnson, Byron Scott, and James Worthy of the Los Angeles Lakers; not Larry Bird, Kevin McHale or Danny Ainge of the Boston Celtics. When I played football I was Lynn Swan, John Stallworth or Terry Bradshaw of my favorite NFL team the Pittsburgh Steelers. Okay, Terry is white, but what the heck, I'm not racist against white people either so leave me alone.

I'm so glad that I didn't hear racist language in my own house growing up. I'm glad I wasn't taught to be a racist at home, even if my grandfather tried once a week. Racism is learned at various points in our lives. I think we all have a little racism in us, even if it's just thinking our ethnicity is the best. I'm Italian, and there isn't anything else I'd rather be. I love the food, I love my big Italian family, and everything that comes along with being Italian. There's no other ethnicity I'd rather be so that automatically makes me slightly racist against all other ethnicities. That's as far as it goes for me though. I love all people, and I feel that everybody has amazing cultural gifts to offer. My best friend is Arab and I love his family. They are very similar to my own. They are kind, all close with one another, and are always offering you something to eat or drink when you go to their house. Very much like Italians. When I went to prison, and received a sentence that was based on conduct I was found not guilty of, I felt I was denied a constitutional right I was born with. I can only imagine that's how many African Americans often feel. The most famous words in the Declaration of Independence are "We hold these truths to be self-evident, that all men are created equal; that they are endowed by their Creator with certain unalienable Rights, that among these are Life, Liberty, and the pursuit of Happiness." Last night I went to see The BlacKkKlansman with my good friend Michael Esposito. The movie wasn't great, and started out slow, but the last 30 minutes were very good, and the last two minutes or so were extremely powerful, and almost brought a tear to my eye.

Here we are 242 years after slave owner Thomas Jefferson wrote those famous words in the Declaration of Independence, and I'm watching a clip of racist, white nationalists marching in a 'Unite the Right' rally in Charlottesville. I watched the rage-filled James Alex Fields drive his car into a crowd killing Heather Heyer. They also showed clips of Donald Trump shamefully talking about the march, and referring to the Neo Nazis as "good people". The ending was sad, and everyone in the theater walked out in silence. It's so sad that all these years later some groups in America still do not have the same right to "Life, Liberty, and the pursuit of Happiness" because clearly many Americans do not believe all men are created equal. Maybe that was inevitable when even after the death of the declaration's author, 130 of those enslaved at Jefferson's Monticello plantation were sold from an auction block. We certainly have come far, but holy shit, not near far enough.

An issue I couldn't wait to address was the NFL's kneeling controversy. To me, this was such an important topic, and all you had to do was scroll down your Facebook wall for 30 seconds to see how it is on so many of your ignorant friend's minds. I would constantly see different memes or statements on how, if they see these spoiled, rich athletes taking a knee they won't watch the NFL again, etc. etc. etc., (well unless their team is winning, then they will watch). First off, let me say, if I were African American, I'm not so sure I would ever stand for the National Anthem for a country which has never afforded me equal protection under the law. In the end that's what all this boils to; equal protection under the law. First off, the National Anthem itself was written by a racist, and has an extremely racist third verse which was removed. The third verse of the Star-Spangled Banner goes as follows "and where is the band who so vauntingly swore, that havoc of war and the battle's confusion a home and a country should leave us no more? Their blood has wash'd out their foul footstep's pollution. No Refuge could save the hireling and slave, from the terror of flight or the gloom of the grave, and the star-spangled banner in triumph doth wave, o'er the land of the free and the home of the brave." Author Frances Key Scott was a DC prosecutor who believed anyone who possessed abolitionist literature should receive the death penalty. That's a bit hard Frances. So, this is the song that you expect African Americans should stand at attention for? Most people aren't even aware of that racist verse. The full version or the history behind the full version of the Star-Spangled Banner certainly isn't taught to us in school.

Now let's briefly run through the history of African Americans in the United States, and see if we can find a time where they have enjoyed this all important concept of equal protection under the law. This won't even be close to a full history, and will leave many important people and events out. This book isn't written for historians, it's written to give the average person a nice overview so they can see where America has been, to say the least, imperfect. This is somewhat debatable as to whether or not the 19 Africans brought to Jamestown, Virginia in 1619 by Dutch traders were slaves or indentured servants, but I think as far as painting a picture of African Americans journey in the U.S. we can start here. So from the early 1600's to the passing of the Thirteenth Amendment in December of 1865 African Americans were slaves. Technically with Abraham Lincoln's Emancipation Proclamation in 1863, slavery was effectively ended, but again for painting the picture we don't need to get caught up in every detail. After slavery ended, we have the failed Reconstruction era, which ended with the Compromise of 1877. When I write "failed" that's not to say the Reconstruction era was a complete failure with no successes, but it ended far too soon and with far too many promises left unfulfilled. If the 'Forty acres and a mule' promise was fulfilled, newly freed slaves would have had land, and wealth to pass down to their children. Instead, almost all land allocated during the war was restored to its pre-war owners. The whole plight of African Americans could have been different. Black Codes were brought about in late 1865 in Mississippi and South Carolina. Mississippi kept newly freed slaves down by requiring black individuals to have written evidence of employment for the coming year every January. If these newly "free" people left before that year's contract was completed they would have to forfeit wages already earned or be arrested. South Carolina also had Black Codes in the form of laws which forbade black people from having any job other than being a farmer or a servant. If somehow any newly freed black person did get a job outside of these two areas they were forced to pay an annual tax of anywhere from $10.00 to $100.00 dollars. Black people were often charged with vagrancy and made to work right back on a plantation. So much for freedom.

After the Reconstruction Era, African Americans, as you could imagine, still had a difficult time finding work; thus many African Americans remained sharecroppers or tenant farmers. Basically, they were back to where they started with being indentured servants or perhaps slaves minus the slave drivers. Segregation continued with Jim Crow laws, and the Supreme Court's 1896 ruling in Plessy v. Ferguson of "separate but equal." Throughout this time as African Americans struggled to find any economic stability, and dealt with separate but equal, they also had to contend with the severe violence of the KKK. Founded in 1866, the KKK was everywhere in the South by the 1870s, and it wasn't like those who fled to the Northern States were living fantastic, prejudice-free lives while receiving amazing educations so they could prosper and be accepted as equals. The height of both the KKK's membership and violence was in the 1920's with lynchings, beatings, and burning crosses commonplace. African Americans lived in both fear, and poverty.

WWII brought some hope and relief to African Americans simply because there was a demand for labor, and military service. Hope for those who served came in the thought that if they served their country, then their country would accept them as equals upon their return..... not exactly, sorry. Voter suppression continued with only 2% of Southern African Americans being registered to vote, but that slowly began to rise and hit about 12% in 1947. Still, 12% is not exactly having your voice heard, and voting itself was always met with both violence, and laws to make it nearly impossible. Then we have the civil rights era from 1954 to 1968 with the culmination being the passing of the July 2nd 1964 Civil Rights Act by then President Lyndon Johnson. There were many notable achievements and milestones during the civil rights era. The civil rights era saw Rosa Parks thrust into the movement, and with the help of many including Martin Luther King Jr who organized the boycott of the Montgomery bus system. Due to continued voter suppression, President Dwight Eisenhower signed the Civil Rights Act of 1957, allowing federal prosecution of anyone who tried to prevent someone from voting. In August of 1963, over 200,000 people marched on Washington, D.C. with Martin Luther King Jr. making his famous "I have a dream" speech. This August of 1963 march is the exact thing that is needed to change our current "lock every African American up in prison" policies. Again, another voting rights act was needed because voter suppression was still running rampant in the south. President Johnson signed the Voting Rights Act of 1965 which banned all voter literacy tests, and provided federal examiners in various jurisdictions. Finally, the Fair Housing Act of 1968 made it illegal to discriminate in housing based on race, sex, national origin or religion. As I wrote about earlier, housing discrimination was still something African Americans had to deal with and segregation was always at the heart of the matter because many white Americans did not want African Americans living in the same neighborhoods as they resided.

Now we are moving into the 1970's which isn't exactly ancient history. Although federally funded segregated housing began with Roosevelt and the New Deal, the 1970's saw an explosion of Section 8 project-based housing. Segregation is always something our government has been keen on, and really still is to this very day. Integration was fought even in the North with some of the most violent protests about school integration taking place in Boston. Underfunded schools with no resources were a constant theme for generations of African Americans. African Americans made many strides politically, socially, and economically throughout the 1970's and 1980's. In 1971, there were only 8 African American mayors, but by the mid-1970's there were 135 total. Unfortunately, the 1970's began a new form of segregation which continues today. Our government's new form of segregation is moving African Americans from their inner city housing units to prisons.

The 1980's also saw the crack epidemic which was spurred along by Reagan and the CIA's involvement with the Contras. Prior to the mid-1980's the average prison sentence for African Americans was six percent higher than whites, but by 1990 the average sentence for African Americans was over 90% higher than whites. This was due in large part to the sentencing differences for powdered cocaine compared to crack cocaine. Segregation continued to be the theme for African Americans in America, and the 1990's were no different. In New York State, 80% of African American children attended predominantly underfunded black schools. Lack of education leads to lack of opportunities, and lack of success.

Bill Clinton's Presidency saw the implementation of draconian drug laws including the three strikes you're out crime bill. President Clinton put 100,000 more police officers on the streets and admittedly "locked up minor actors for way too long." It's easy for a politician like Bill Clinton to admit their mistake after the fact, but I don't in any way think these decisions weren't made not knowing exactly what was going to be the result. His policies helped create more jobs for one segment of the population while locking up another. Incarceration numbers in recent years have gone down slowly with the States leading the way. President Obama did far too little with the only reforms being passed during his administration being the 2010 Fair Sentencing Act, which reduced crack-cocaine penalties, and the Second Chance Pell Pilot Program, which allowed incarcerated Americans to receive Pell Grants to pursue post-secondary education programs.

Under President Trump, racism has moved more out in the open again, but hopefully now that Mr. Trump is out of office things will get a little better. Trump understood he could lead the rhetoric that many racists love, whether it's about NFL players kneeling or police brutality. I'm not saying the police are always wrong, but certainly the prospect of being shot and killed even while doing what you're instructed to do is real for many African Americans; especially African American males. For easy viewing, I'm going to put a brief bullet point history of why if African American athletes feel they need to respectfully take a knee to shed light on social injustices, you should shut the fuck up and try having some empathy.

-1619 to 1865, Slavery
-1865 to 1877, Failed Reconstruction
-1877 to 1950's, Jim Crow, Separate but Equal and massive KKK led violence
-1954 to 1968 The Civil Rights Era saw progress, poverty, and more violence
-1970 to Present, continued segregation through leased housing, and the start of mass incarceration which continues to this very day
-Lock them up, lock them up, lock them up

If you are white, can you imagine going through all that violence, and discrimination simply because the color of your skin is darker than the color of someone else's skin? It's so simple; solely because their skin color is darker, they have endured murder, rape, slavery, segregation, and fear. African Americans along with many of their white brothers and sisters (kind of stealing that from one of my heroes Cornel West) fought tooth-and-nail for every right they have today. Again, if you're white can you imagine having to fight for every right that others were just born with? Can you imagine being somewhere, and wondering if someone dislikes you for no other reason than the color of your skin? Can you imagine being pulled over on a dark night, and having the thought of wanting to make sure you do everything right because you know the situation could escalate, and you could end up in jail or dead? Can you imagine never once having equal protection under the law? Can you imagine not being able to respectfully take a knee in silent protest with tons of people flipping out, and acting as if you have no reason or right to respectfully protest just because you're an athlete who makes a lot of money? First off, that is the exact reason they should be taking a knee. NFL or NBA players have the forum to bring attention to an issue that's important to them. If they were Joe the bus driver taking a knee would anyone care? No, of course fucking not. I wasn't a big Kaepernick fan as a QB, but certainly he's good enough to at least be the backup for almost all NFL teams. The reason Kaepernick isn't playing in the NFL is because he's clearly being black balled. Anyway, if you don't understand why NFL players should be able to take a knee you're either ignorant or racist. Which one are you?

Racism has certainly changed. Prospects for achievements by African Americans are better than ever. If you are growing up as a black male or maybe even some females may disagree with that statement, but go talk to your grandparents or any elder in your family, and I'm sure they will agree with me for the most part. Today's racist looks different from the one of years past. Today's racist looks like some of my old friends on Facebook, who aren't really my friends anymore. Today's racist looks like some of my family members. Today's racist, in my opinion, isn't as bold faced, violent, or dangerous as in years past. Although, like I wrote earlier, Trump has reinvigorated, and embolden racist behavior to be more out in the open, but like everything, time will change that. In general, today's racist will be kind to your face, and talk shit behind your back. Today's racist will hire you to work for them, but then if their employment doesn't work out they may blame it on the color of your skin while using the N word to their close friends. Today's racist can judge you as an individual. Nevertheless, today's racists have a poor opinion of the African American race on the whole, with no understanding of how history directly ties into some of their present struggles.

If throughout the history of a certain group of people, that group was continually denied access to opportunities and resources, how would you expect that group to have the same level of success as another group? Kids born from educated, wealthy parents are going to grow up, and become educated, wealthy adults. The process continues generation after generation because they are afforded completely different opportunities than a kid who was born into a family that is poor, and uneducated. Being born to poor, uneducated parents doesn't mean you can't achieve, but it certainly makes it more difficult. Then throw centuries of discrimination into the mix and see where you end up. I always say if life is a marathon then if you're a black male you're often starting out 50 yards behind the end of the pack. There is nothing genetically inferior about an African American, a Latino American, or any other race when comparing them to another. Part of the problem with today's racist is he doesn't see oppression like he once saw in the history books. I try to explain to people that time doesn't exist in a bubble. When talking about the difficulties faced today, you have to tie it into yesterday, and the yesterday before that, and so on till you get to the beginning. Then you should be able to draw the line between today, and yesterday, and see that it's all interconnected, and maybe instead of feeling anger when you see someone taking a knee, you will have empathy and compassion.

The Black Lives Matter movement started out on shaky ground for me. The Black Lives Matter movement started out as the hashtag #BlackLivesMatter after George Zimmerman's acquittal of killing Trayvon Martin. It's not that under normal circumstances I didn't think George Zimmerman shouldn't have been convicted, but the stupid ass State of Florida has a stupid ass "stand your ground" law. The Stand Your Ground law needs to be done away with, it's ridiculous, and has no place in our world. If you are defending yourself then you can use a "Self Defense" defense. Stand Your Ground takes that defense to another level, as well as taking stupidity to another level. The real problem in this case isn't that George Zimmerman was acquitted under Florida's current law, but that Mr. Zimmerman was racially motivated to protect his community from what he perceived as a threat based simply on the fact that Trayvon Martin was black. If Trayvon was white, Mr. Zimmerman probably still would have watched him initially, but then Mr. Zimmerman would have figured the person was walking home or to a friend's house, and let him be. However, because Trayvon Martin was black Mr. Zimmerman assumed the worst, and because Mr. Zimmerman assumed the worst, Trayvon Martin ended up dead.

The Black Lives Matter movement is something I understand the need for, and support, but it's also something that needs some changes. The need for those changes makes me less vocal in my support. There are times like when Charleston, South Carolina Police Officer, Michael T. Slager shot/murdered a fleeing Walter L. Scott where Black Lives Matter needs to be there protesting. When something like that happens, I always think, "can you imagine how many times something like that was done, and not filmed, and the cop lied about it?" If that wasn't caught on cell phone video, that Police Officer would have lied, and said Mr. Scott attacked him, and tried to get his gun, or he would have planted a gun on him, and he would have gotten away with murder. Throughout the years that's happened thousands of times, and when it happens, Police need to be held accountable, just as any citizen would. Furthermore, other Police Officers need to call that person out instead of defending their actions. I see horrible conduct consistently defended by officers when a fellow officer gets caught doing something wrong. Many times CNN or some other news organization will interview some retired captain or an officer, and instead of calling out their fellow officer, he or she defends them. It's disgusting, and does them no good.

On the other hand, I don't think it was clear that, in the Ferguson shooting of Michael Brown, the Police Officer was in the wrong. Maybe he was, but from everything I've read it seems Officer Darren Wilson may have been justified in shooting Mr. Brown. There are problems on both sides in this instance though. Perhaps Black Lives Matter should have some sort of waiting period to let some facts come out before protests begin. I think when protests begin right away then details come out where the individual is on drugs, and or attacked the officer then it puts in question the movement's credibility in many people's eyes. On the other hand the U.S. Department of Justice released a report that showed racial discrimination at disturbing levels so it's a wonder why the mistrust of Police was at a level where waiting wasn't even part of their thought process. Federal officials learned that city officials worked together with law enforcement to generate as much money as possible from fines and court fees. This often helps keep lower income people poor and desperate, and then if they can't pay their fines they end up in jail. Hmmm, I kind of remember reading a similar tactic that was done in 1865 in Mississippi, and South Carolina. Do you remember reading it? I hope so, it was only a couple pages ago. In Ferguson, the city relied on the police department and the courts to generate revenue to fill budget gaps. Racial profiling seemed to be rampant in the Ferguson Police Department where from 2012 to 2014, 85% of individuals who were pulled over were African American. The most telling issue that shows severe prejudice is when African Americans were pulled over they were almost 2 ½ times more likely to be searched, leading to 93% of those arrested being black even though white individuals were more likely to have contraband. Personally, I don't think anyone should be able to be searched when pulled over. It's more bullshit about how we are the freest country in the world, yet I can't go two blocks without seeing a police vehicle. I'm not sure how it is with State Troopers in other states but in New York they seem to exist solely to write tickets to pay their own salaries. State troopers not only write tickets on the NY State thruway, but they come into the poor cities of Niagara Falls and Buffalo and write tickets, which is completely ridiculous. State troopers coming into poor cities truly hurts the local population's ability to spend money at local restaurants, and contribute to the local economy in general. It's not as if State Troopers come in and help local police by responding to a domestic call or something more pressing. No, State Troopers exist solely to generate money for themselves and the State.

If a police officer murders someone, the officer needs to be charged, and then convicted just like the rest of us would be. Part of the problem is that everyone in the justice system are all on the same team. You don't see members of the same football team tackling their own running back, well, unless they play for the Cleveland Browns, then they might. First off, it's almost impossible for an officer to get indicted, so if they do, you can bet the prosecutor must have had no choice in the matter. More than likely if an officer was indicted it was caught on film, and therefore it was followed by public outcry. Then, the prosecutor and their team got together to see if there was any way possible they could not indict the officer. This attempt not to charge the officer is the complete opposite of what they do when it's a public citizen. Nearly every year police officers kill approximately 1,000 people. That's a lot of dead people. I'm sure the officers in many or most cases are in the right or had no choice, but I'm also sure that in many instances they did not have to kill the person.

Let's take the murder of 40 year old Terence Crutcher. Tulsa Oklahoma police officer Betty Shelby murdered Mr. Crutcher, and I don't care what anyone else says because they are full of shit. I watched the YouTube video many times, and there is no way in hell that Betty Shelby needed to kill Mr. Crutcher. Officer Shelby had another officer right beside her, and there were at least four officers on the scene because two more were right behind her. Not to mention it was 45 minutes before someone finally approached Terence Crutcher's body to administer any type of CPR, and although I'm not a doctor, I'm pretty sure it was a little too late for that. Umm, thanks for trying though??? Do you know when it's a pretty good indication the officer was completely wrong for killing a black guy? If you guessed when Donald Trump would come out and say so, you would be correct. Mr. Trump stated that the video had him feeling "very, very troubled." Mr. Trump went on to state "That man went to the car, hands up, put his hand on the car. I mean, to me, it looked like he did everything he's supposed to do." Come on, even Donald Trump is saying you, a black guy, did everything right, and his family still can't get justice. So what happened when Officer Shelby went to trial? The same thing that happens many times when officers go to trial, Officer Shelby was acquitted. That's complete bullshit, and if Betty Shelby wasn't a cop she would be in prison right now, plain, and simple.

The number of people killed by police officers is pretty consistently close to 1,000 a year, and between 2005 and 2017, 80 officers had been arrested for either murder or manslaughter. The bar is set pretty high for an officer to be charged in the first place so I would assume that of those 80 officers at least 90% were convicted. Well, you know what they say about how you should never assume. I guess they made an ass out of me because only about 35% of those 80 police officers were convicted. Most, like Officer Shelby, were acquitted and then went back to work on the force. If you're a regular citizen in the real world and you go to trial, the conviction rate jumps up to 92%. As my awesome Uncle Sal always says "Un-fucking believable." Actually, I've never even heard my Uncle Sal swear before, but he is awesome.

Unfortunately, like anytime power is transferred or given to someone that power is often abused or used to enrich themselves and it appears that has happened with the BLM movement. All sorts of problems are arising and faith in those involved with BLM at top levels are dwindling. From accusations of funneling millions of dollars in donations into personal accounts to the article in New York Magazine which reported leaders purchasing property in Southern California for approximately $6 million dollars. BLM also used an $8 million dollar grant to purchase property in Toronto. Leaders stated the $6 million dollar home in Los Angeles is used as a safe house and for black creators. There is the usual nepotism as with anything. For example Patrisse Cullors was one of the leaders of BLM, brother helps run the house and is paid with BLM funds. To be honest the whole thing is quite confusing and for those donating or who want to support the BLM movement it can be really confusing. Black Lives Matter and Black Lives Matter Global Network Foundation are two separate organizations and have no association with one another. Black Lives Matter Global has raised over 90 million dollars since 2020, and according to an article written in The Moguldom Nation by Ann Brown more than 10.6 billion dollars have been donated to BLM causes since 2013. I'm sure many who have donated assumed all the BLM organizations were one in the same, but that's not the case. The BLM original founders, Alicia Garza, Patrisse Cullors, and Opal Tometi have been accused of not putting a single donated dollar into the hands of poor black individuals. I've always thought it was crazy whether you are talking about BLM or a cause we all donated to the Red Cross over wouldn't the money be better off given directly to the people who need it? You always see billions of dollars donated yet nothing ever changes on the ground for anyone. How can we not assume there is massive funneling of funds in all these situations. Patrisse Cullors was the Executive Director and did use the Los Angeles home to shoot a number of her personal YouTube videos. BLMGNF is the largest and the most well funded of the BLM movements. So in general BLM is decentralized and each BLM chapter differs in organization, structure, tactics, and fundraising. Therefore if you are going to donate, do your own research and make sure you are donating to a chapter who you fully support.

Black Lives Matter is needed because we all recognize the fact that All Lives Matter, but it's painfully obvious America has not completely realized that "black lives" are included in "all lives." I'm pretty sure no other group of people would love it more than black people if there were no need to have a Black Lives Matter movement. Well, except for those who have personally financially gained from BLM fundraising success. The movement isn't perfect. Clearly a reorganizing of the movement needs to take place. Also, as I stated, I would like to see a waiting period before protests begin. If a Police Officer is clearly in the right then I would like to see Black Lives Matter come out with a statement in support of the police. Black Lives Matter has a network now with over 40 chapters so I'm sure it's difficult to organize, but I'd like to see Black Lives Matter come together and address various other problems within the black community, and not just to protest during the times of police brutality. So many black individuals along with Black Twiter really stepped up to get justice for Shanquella Robinson. This case really bothered me and I felt so horrible for this girl. Shanquella went to Cabo with individuals whom she thought were her friends. Unfortunately the 25 year old died on October 29th 2022 at the hands of at least one of these horrible people while the others filmed it, watched and not one of these weak, horrible people did anything to help. Furthermore after Shanquella had died these individuals tried to cover up the death and not only lied to authorities, but came back to the U.S. and lied to Shanquella's family. Many Youtube channels posted videos daily demanding justice for Shanquella, but I searched and could not find one instance of BLM demanding justice for someone who needs justice every bit as much as anyone.

The debate on black-on-black crime seems to be a contentious issue on both sides. I've heard racist people speak about it with no acknowledgement of the issues that cause it. I've also heard African Americans speak about it, and basically deny it's an issue or say it's racist to even bring it up, which is both counterproductive, and ridiculous. Before I get into the subject, I want to be clear in my thought that black-on-black crime is a completely separate issue from an officer of the law killing an unarmed African American, or a White American for that matter. Police are killing far too many people in general. In 2016, police officers shot and killed 50 unarmed black people, and they also shot and killed 50 unarmed white people. It's actually true that more white people are shot and killed by the police every year, but when you take population numbers into consideration, African Americans are 2 ½ times more likely to be killed by the police than white Americans. Police officers are agents of the state who are paid to protect and serve so you shouldn't have to ever worry about being shot for little or no reason at all. Anyway, those are two separate issues, and I don't think it's fair if we are talking about the number of unarmed black people shot by police to say, "yeah but more black people died by other black people killing them." So, that makes it okay? No, of course it doesn't, and that's one of the reasons they are separate issues, and have no business being lumped together.

Black-on-black crime is real though, just as white-on-white crime is real. The recurring theme of segregation and poverty are the main causes, but there are also other issues that need to be addressed. The reason white people commit crimes against other white people is they tend to live in white neighborhoods. The same reason applies to black people who commit crimes against other black people, because they often live in neighborhoods that are primarily black. The issue of black on black or white on white crime isn't exactly rocket science as to how it happens that way, but it's also not so simple that we can just end the conversation right there either. It is as simple as proximity as far as why it's white-on-white or black-on-black crime, but the amount of crimes or why those crimes are committed are different.

I read an article from October, 2017 in The Root by Michael Harriot titled "Why We Never Talk About Black-on-Black Crime: An Answer to White America's Most Pressing Question." I was a little surprised because in my opinion Mr. Harriot came off as very racist in the article. In the last two years, I unfriended 5 white people for racist comments, and 4 black people for their racist comments. I write this because I will not put up with racism no matter who or where it comes from. Even the title itself was offensive, "An Answer to White America's Most Pressing Question." First off, it's not white America's most pressing question by any stretch of the imagination, and for most of us if we are speaking about that subject it's because we care. Unless you're a Fox News viewer, Trump supporting racist, the question of black-on-black crime is asked to find out what can be done to solve it, not to place blame. An early point I reject from Mr. Harriot's article is "It's not a thing." The reason Mr. Harriot uses as to why it's not a thing is because white-on-white crime exists. Well, just because one thing exists, it doesn't mean the other does not exist. The two issues don't cancel each other out. It just means they both exist. Shootings kill more than 36,000 Americans every year. That means close to 100 people every single day are killed by being shot. An even more startling figure is between 2001 and 2014; 440,095 people were killed by firearms in the United States.

Mass shootings are defined differently by different organizations, thus their statistics vary greatly. The non-profit organization Gun Violence Archive defines mass shootings by four or more individuals either killed or wounded by a shooter in one incident. The liberal magazine Mother Jones defines mass shootings as "a single attack in a public place in which three or more victims were killed." In 2017, there were 273 shootings that met the criteria set by Gun Violence Archive. The data on who commits the majority of mass shootings ranges depending on the study with a study done by Mother Jones putting the percentage at 54% committed by whites while Grant Duwe, author of "Mass Murder in the United States: A History" puts it at 63%. Mr. Duwe does go all the way back to 1900, while Mother Jones's study only went back to 1982. It's actually insane that something in our control is killing close to 100 people a day, and yet we do nothing about it. Gun violence is a huge problem concerning white-on-white crime, and black-on-black crime. Concerning gun related deaths, White Americans are more often involved in mass shootings, shootings of their spouse, and suicides. African Americans deaths relating to gun violence are vastly different than was described concerning white gun violence. According to the Centers for Disease Control and Prevention, African Americans are eight times more likely to be shot and killed by guns than white Americans are. Even though African Americans are only about 13% of the population, black individuals are killed more by guns in all 50 states; African Americans account for 51%

of all homicide victims in America. Mr. Harriot's second point of "It has nothing to do with what we are talking about," only makes sense if you are trying to talk about police violence, and someone dismisses that just because there is black on black crime. As I stated, they are two separate issues. Mr. Harriot writes "Imagine the head of Homeland Security walking up to the microphone to hold a press conference after a horrific terrorist attack, but when reporters start asking him about stopping terrorism and catching the culprits, he begins talking about texting and driving." It's an over the top analogy that isn't helpful in the discussion about black-on-black crime.

I do agree with Mr. Harriot when he writes "It is true that the vast majority of black murders are committed by black men, and we should do something to combat that statistic, but that fact has nothing to do with state violence." I completely agree, and stated so earlier as well, but that doesn't mean myself or others should be shouted down on the issue of black-on-black violence.

African American Pastors, and community activists often get shouted down when they use the terminology of "black-on-black crime" as if they are betraying their race. Those individuals shouldn't be silenced, and nor should I. Instead, you should have titled your article something to do with what your third point was about in "We actually do talk about it… all the time." Mr. Harriot points out that "there are countless organizations, activists and movements dedicated to curbing violence in black communities" which is awesome. What Mr. Harriot fails to realize is that most white people are aware of this, and often are out there trying to help as well. Mr. Harriot also insinuates that white people wouldn't know any of this and writes "there's no way white people would know about this unless they stopped deflecting with trite questions and instead actually went into minority neighborhoods to selflessly join the effort to address the problems plaguing…" Ok, you can stop laughing now. Wow, as if millions of white people haven't fought alongside black people to further their cause. As if white people weren't instrumental in the abolitionist movement. As if white people didn't march along with Martin Luther King Jr. during the civil rights era. As if white people don't support the Black Lives Matter movement. There are millions of racist white people out there, but there are millions more who love all people. One thing I am begging black people to stop doing is lumping all "white people" in one category as if we are all Trump supporting racists. It's insulting, and I hear it all the time.

D.L. Hughley, who is both funny as hell, and very intelligent was on a recent Bill Maher episode, and multiple times when talking about something negative, says "white people" this and "white people" that. Fuck, at least say "some white people" I don't want to be lumped in with racist white people, who are in the minority any more than you want to be lumped in with something negative about black people. The last thing I will point out is how Mr. Harriot feels just because someone is white "It ain't none of their damn business." You know what, fuck white nationalists, fuck David Duke, and those red necks who are keeping the KKK alive, fuck people who refuse to acknowledge systematic racist policies that make success much more difficult for African Americans, fuck Fox Fake News, Fuck Kellyanne Conway, fuck Tucker Carlson, fuck the corporations, fuck the lobbyists, fuck the Republican Congress, especially Lindsey (Linda) Graham, fuck Donald J. Trump, fuck the Republican and Democrat Parties, and you know what, fuck you too Michael Harriot, you're not helping either.

Conclusion

We are all products of our environment and I don't think ODB was correct when said "it's all good in the hooooood." Aristotle said "Give me a child until he is 7 and I will show you the man." I used to work at an elementary school in the inner city in Niagara Falls, NY. There is a great mix of kids there with many of the kids being African American. One of the kindergarten teachers had a baby so I ended up subbing in that classroom for quite a while. It was crazy because even though the kids were just beginning their academic careers, I felt like they were already so far behind they were never going to be able to catch up. Most of the kids couldn't recognize more than a few letters. The students couldn't spell their own names. I got to work with the kids one-on-one much of the time because even in kindergarten the kids had state testing. I would act really dramatic when they got something correct, and I would tell them how smart they were and fall down on the ground because I was so amazed. Their little faces would just light up, and they were so proud of themselves. Job wise, it was one of the most rewarding experiences I've ever had. I used to get entire kindergarten classes running up to me in the hall trying to hug me when I wasn't in their class. They were such great kids. I subbed in that school for a couple of years, and the change that took place in these kids from kindergarten to 3rd grade was fairly drastic. Their environment had already started to have a negative influence on them. Everything from the way they spoke to their behavior. The environment these kids are growing up in is beyond their control yet it forms so much of their life. Segregation, and poverty again are the continued themes.

Many single mothers do a fantastic job raising their sons or daughters, and often get some much needed family help from grandma or grandpa. However, to say it's not an issue at all would be to ignore the issue. 66% of all African American families are single parent families, while the National average is 40%. African males need to do a better job in being fathers, and/or giving financial support. African American leaders need to do a better job as well. There are so many legitimate reasons why African Americans have it more difficult than individuals who are white. Yet here we are. So, what can we do? We can't go back in time, and do all the things that should have been done. I wish we could, obviously we wouldn't have slavery to begin with. If we couldn't make that change, and started after slavery we could have given African Americans land, proper employment, education, and thus the ability to have upward mobility. The ability to advance for African Americans has been fought tooth-and-nail every step of the way. Unfortunately, we can't go back in time one second let alone years. So let's start from here.

How about mentors in school from kindergarten through 12th grade? The mentorship can start in kindergarten or in the 1st grade, and continue throughout their academic careers. Yeah, I know you're already thinking about the cost, but I'm pretty sure it would be less than incarcerating those individuals who will be able to make better choices at early ages due to professional mentorships.

Yes, professional mentorships; now this is a jobs program I can get behind. Instead of the immoral incarceration jobs program, let's have a moral mentorship jobs program. The entire society would benefit, well except for the prison industrial complex, but you we can easily add them to my list of "fuck you." They should have been in there any way. So, correction officers, judges, and the whole prison industrial complex, a big fuck you too. There, I feel so much better now.

In the past, our government has contributed to segregation through various policies. However, people also self-segregate. When I attended the University at Buffalo I would often meet my brother Mark, and my friends Pete Casler, and Tony Kutis to get something to eat while on a break. I would look around, and be blown away how much everyone segregated themselves. There was literally a distinct white area, a black area, and an Asian area. There was obviously some cross mixing, especially with black and white students, but still for the most part if you were from a certain race, and maybe didn't know many people, you would go sit in the section where people look similar to you. It was the same way in prison as well. This also applies to where people move to. In recent years there have been HUD programs to help integrate people, but often individuals tend to move to areas they are familiar with. The issue with living in those traditionally poor, segregated neighborhoods compared to moving to a suburb is moving to a better neighborhood often leads to better outcomes. If you look at employment rates, earning rates, school test scores, children born to unwed mothers, the outcomes for black families living in integrated neighborhoods improve. Also, for me the more important issue is what the young kids are seeing and not seeing, growing up in one area compared to another.

I worked in sales and marketing for low income seniors. If I had to estimate I would think approximately 60% of the people I've met have been white, 30% black, and 10% Hispanic. All the individuals I've met lived in some sort of low income, subsidized housing, and they have all been segregated. If I meet with a white person, they live among mostly white people. If I met with a black person, they live mostly among black people. Hispanics also lived among other Hispanics, but at least from my experience Hispanics are more integrated as far as where they live. Other than where Hispanics live they usually stick around each other because many of the Hispanics who are seniors speak little to no English. Of the better outcomes for African Americans; I'm certain we can add African Americans growing up in the suburbs will also be less likely to be arrested. We are nearing the mid

2020s, segregation, whether self-imposed or government encouraged, needs to end.

When concerning racial prejudice, I'm truly hopeful for the future. With each passing generation racism becomes less and less prevalent. Think back to my grandfather's generation where racist attitudes were the norm. I doubt my mother would have been able to bring a little black girlfriend over to her house like I was able to bring a black, and a Puerto Rican friend over. I'm close with an ex-girlfriend's son who is black, and he has lots of friends who are of all different races. The melting pot theory first surfaced in the late 1700's, but never really fully took place with African Americans. I think this is the century the melting pot is truly taking place. In 1970, only 1% of the population was multi-racial. Today, over 10% of the population is multi-racial. Furthermore, according to Pew the multi-racial population in the United States is growing at a rate three times faster than any other population group in the entire country. As interracial marriage and children continue to rise, prejudice will continue to fall. It's inevitable, but the governmental segregation policy of locking up African Americans is the one issue that will derail all the positives we are all trying to accomplish. Locking African Americans up makes it easy for racist attitudes to feel like they are justified in their racism. Locking African Americans up at young ages makes it nearly impossible to ever become a productive member of society, and holds back African Americans more than anything else.

As I stated earlier, there needs to be a civil rights era type of movement concerning this policy. Locking up African Americans is something our government does on purpose, and many who are participating are not even aware because it's been the norm for so long people who are willing or unwilling participants don't even understand. Individuals such as It doesn't seem that anyone in our government is going to take the lead so in large part it needs to be an issue the public takes on and maybe this would be a great issue for BLM to tackle. It is also important the media keeps the story in the news cycle so it won't just be buried like the souls of countless locked up individuals.

Chapter 6-

The Cancer Conspiracy

It seems nowadays everyone knows multiple people who have cancer, or have died from cancer. Was it always this way? I never heard any of my friend's grandparents dying of cancer. As a matter of fact, in 1900, cancer and heart disease combined accounted for less than 18% of all deaths in the United States. These days, heart disease and cancer account for just under 50% of all deaths in America. My grandmother on my mothers side lived to 95 and my grandfather on my father's side also lived to 95, and it was a fall that did him in or I think he would have lived to see triple digits.

I wasn't so lucky as to see my father live to 95. My father passed away from cancer at 66. Certainly not a tragedy in that he died young, but it was still too young as far as I was concerned. My father was the toughest guy I ever heard of let alone knew. I remember as a kid my father having a tooth that needed to come out, but there was no way this man was going to take a day off of work to go to the dentist. I watched my father take a pair of pliers and pull out his tooth, and thought, "he's fucking crazy." My father's toughness came from within in that if something needed to be done there was really nothing that stopped him. Even as an older man he was still a beast. One day at work a 150 pound machine came crashing down on him, breaking his foot. My father again refused to take even an hour off of work so he laced his boot up tight, and went back to work. I'm not saying that was smart, but because his toughness was at some super power level to me, I never in a million years thought something could kill him like cancer did. Yet cancer indeed did kill my father. My father dwindled down in weight and while in the hospital waiting to start treatment the cancer inside of him burst in his intestine. I was called to the hospital, but didn't know he was dying until we spoke to the doctor. I went in to see my father and I had tears in my eyes and even though the drugs had started to take over in him he looked at me, sat up somewhat, grabbed my arm and said "don't worry about me." I wish I would have gotten there earlier. I wish I would have spoken to my father and hounded him to go to the doctor, but most of all I wish he didn't die of cancer.

My aunt Margie has cancer. A number of my friends lost loved ones because of cancer, including my really good friends Mark Dardes and Jimmy Andrews. RIP Mr. Andrews, and Michelle. A few of my uncles have had cancer, but none of their parents had cancer. Cancer seems to be omnipresent these days. So what changed? Is cancer just another needed industry in America that makes too much money to bother finding a cure? Who makes money off of it? Is it also similar to the prison and military complexes in that it's another immoral jobs program?

In Western New York we have many cancer treatment centers with the biggest being Roswell Park. Roswell Park is the first cancer treatment center in America. It was founded by Dr. Roswell Park in 1898, and currently the cancer treatment center employs over 3,300 people. Buffalo is a smaller, big city, but there is a Roswell Park type of cancer treatment center in every city across America. There are also thousands of additional smaller oncology centers employing hundreds of thousands of more people. Even though the cancer industry does employ hundreds of thousands of people, the jobs are just a byproduct of the disease. From everything I've read it doesn't appear to be anyone's motivating factor as it is in the prison industrial complex.

Pharmaceutical companies, our government, doctors, scientists and thousands of others seem to be looking for cures and ways to prolong the lives of those who have cancer. That doesn't mean the Pharmaceutical companies themselves aren't mostly motivated by money. I think the proof is in the pudding there. According to the American Cancer Society childhood cancers make up less than 1% of all diagnosed cancers each year. Therefore, it's just not profitable for pharmaceutical companies to invest much money into cures for childhood cancer. The strange thing to me is even the federal government only allocates 4% of their cancer research funding for childhood cancer. Hmmm, wonder if it's because our government is doing exactly what the corporations tell them to do. Can't make money off the dying kids so fuck the dying kids. No, they don't actually say that, but they may as well.

One of the differences between our grandparent's generation, and the generations that followed them, is that our grandparent's generation didn't consume the amount of processed food that we do; at least not for their entire lives. So is it the food or chemical producing industries that somehow benefit from giving us cancer? Winner, winner, chicken dinner! No, don't eat a chicken dinner, chicken is not so good for you my friend. The World Health Organization declared processed meat as a carcinogen, and put meats such as corned beef, lunch meat, jerky, salami, bacon, sausage, and hot dogs in group 1 of cancer causers. Group 1 means it's a 100% certainty processed meat causes cancer. In group 2 we have our red meats such as pork, lamb, and beef, and those classified in group 2 by the World Health Organization, and they probably cause cancer (but most experts agree they definitely do). The most common cancers caused by eating meats are breast, prostate, and colon cancers. When you cook meat, the carcinogenic compounds, heterocyclic amines, and polycyclic aromatic hydrocarbons are formed. Saturated fat, cholesterol, antibiotics, and loads of hormones are in the meat you eat. Doctors are often concerned that people are being prescribed antibiotics too often, and thus the antibiotics are becoming less effective. Well, even with millions of humans being over prescribed antibiotics, the vast majority between 65% and 70% are given to animals, and then ultimately, you're consuming them in your meat. Another carcinogen added to your meat to preserve, and add color are sodium nitrite, and sodium nitrate. Consuming too many of these carcinogens can possibly lead to colorectal cancer, ovarian cancer, stomach cancer, non-Hodgkin lymphoma, leukemia, bladder cancer, pancreatic cancer, esophageal cancer, thyroid cancer, and finally heart disease! Fuck that, I'm not eating meat anymore! Oh wait, I'm already a vegetarian. If you eat meat, and you are unable to give it up completely, you should at least cut down, and you will cut down your chances of getting cancer and other diseases as well. You can thank me later.

I named this chapter The Cancer Conspiracy because honestly I just loved the way the name sounds. However, the fact that these huge corporations want to make us sick is unfortunately not even close to a wacky conspiracy theory. Side note, The Cancer Conspiracy was also a progressive rock band from Burlington, Vermont in the early 2000's. They probably love Bernie. Okay, back to the shitty, immoral, greedy corporations who are poisoning and killing us to make billions of dollars. There is a whole history here which ties these companies together. They are subsidiaries, or former companies who changed their names. They are associated with "old money" powerful families, and corporations, but I found myself going crazy doing all the research, and writing page after page of notes. I decided to limit some of the history, and make everything easy and clear. I also found a lot of information tying the Rockefeller Empire into many of these corporations, but it was hard to pinpoint or verify much of the information so I decided to leave them out of it for the most part as well. You can google how they were associated with I.G. Farben in Germany which is the company from which many of the corporations I'm writing about evolved from. There is so much information, but oftentimes it's this trust or that trust, and then names are thrown in there. It usually makes sense, and it may be true, but there was never any real proof in the reports I read, and it often left me with more questions than answers. I decided to keep it short and simple, giving only information that draws clear lines, and clearly shows how a certain corporation does A, causes B, then sells C to make even more money. No conspiracy here; just real proof.

During World War II, I.G. Farben was the largest chemical manufacturing corporation in the world. I.G. Farben enabled Germany to fight the war, and among other things produced chemicals that helped in the murder of millions. Due to these atrocities a few years after WWII, I.G. Farben was split up. Initially the three corporations it was split up into were Bayer, Hoechst, and BASF with I.G. Farben itself put into liquidation. I.G. Farben's liquidation is a whole other story, but not important to this I guess. Here is a list of many of the corporations that are interconnected into this mess of chemicals, cancer, money, pharmaceuticals, various other chronic diseases, and more and more money. The corporations include: J.P. Morgan Chase, Sanofi, Clariant, Bayer, Agfa, BASF, Nestle, Bristol-Myers Squibb, Roche, Procter and Gamble, DowDuPont, Merck and Co. Inc.

If you're looking for one or two devils, or the worst of the worst here, it's definitely Bayer AG and Nestle. We can start with Bayer AG. I was going to list all of Bayer's subsidiaries until I learned they had 11 pages worth! Bayer manufactures many fungicides, herbicides, insecticides, and pharmaceutical medications. Bayer is all around the globe from their headquarters in their home country of Germany to Dubai, United Arab Emirates, Milan, Italy, Lago, Nigeria, and Misgav, Israel. Bayer added to its impressive evil empire when it purchased Monsanto on June 7th 2018. Bayer's annual revenue is over 35 billion dollars. How does Bayer achieve these numbers, and what makes Bayer so evil? Bayer starts the process in the ground and the process is completed when you're in the ground. We can also repeat the same process for other players like DowDuPont. Bayer/Monsanto first sells their genetically modified seeds to farmers. The genetically engineered seeds are highly resistant to the Roundup herbicide Bayer also sells. There are a number of problems with GE seeds. The original promise by Monsanto of genetically modified seeds requiring less pesticides, and producing higher yields was a nice promise by Monsanto, but unfortunately for the farmers who purchased Monsanto/Bayer's seeds those promises have not come to fruition. Genetically engineered seeds also require much more water to grow, and in areas where fresh water is not so easily available farmers use much more of this precious resource than they should. So the farmer buys the GE seeds from Bayer, then Bayer also sells them the pesticides, herbicides, and fungicides. The most well-known herbicide is glyphosate, known and seen in stores everywhere by its commercial name, Roundup. Glyphosate has been linked to over 40 diseases including the big C, cancer. Glyphosate is a broad spectrum, non-selective systemic herbicide. It is often sprayed on fields prior to planting or on crops genetically modified to resist the chemical glyphosate. Glyphosate is known to disrupt the endocrine system, and the balance of bacteria in the gut. Glyphosate can damage DNA, and can be a cause of cancerous mutations. Glyphosate is not only linked to cancer; glyphosate is also linked to hypertension, stroke, diabetes, Alzheimer's diseases, Parkinson's disease, multiple sclerosis, and end stage renal disease.

As previously stated, GE seeds were sold with the promise to increase food production and reduce costs, and since the opposite has happened, we know the real reason for GE seeds is because it's a package deal with Monsanto/Bayer toxic herbicide Roundup. Bugs have also become more resistant to pesticides so farmers use more and more chemicals to combat this increasing problem. In a 10 year span of using GE seeds compared to

Non-GMO seeds, framers increased use of herbicides by almost 500 million pounds. Bayer sells such a massive list of pesticides, herbicides and fungicides there's no point in documenting them all here, and to be honest all the chemicals have similar health consequences. For example, the product Confidor contains the active ingredient Imidacloprid, which in high doses in rats led to death, locomotor issues, cardiovascular effects, liver damage, thyroid damage, reproductive toxicity, developmental retardation, neurobehavioral deficits and as always cancer. It should be noted that various studies including the EPA show Imidacloprid does not cause cancer, while others show Imidacloprid indeed does. It also it should be noted that Imidacloprid is considered non-carcinogenic by the EPA, but fuck the EPA, I don't trust those paid off bastards anyway. Most processed foods include GMO ingredients and 90% of corn, soy, cotton, canola, and sugar beet acreage in the United States are all GMO.

There are many health risks concerning the consumption of GMO foods. Some studies performed on the animals that consume GMO's found such issues as: increased allergies, infertility, organ function issues, gastrointestinal issues, and issues with the body's ability to regulate its insulin production. There are also studies out there that potentially link GMO's with autism. I think common sense should tell us that the changes in our food must have a direct link to the staggering rise in autism rates. Growing up, autism was rare. In 2008 1 in 54 boys were diagnosed with autism and that number continues to increase with the number dropping to 1 in 37 boys in 2018. I'm sure you're wondering, the 2018 number for girls is 1 in every 151 girls; much better but I'm sure we all think it's still too many. Farmers who feed GMO corn to their pigs report seeing behaviors very similar to the traits of autistic children. Studies performed on rats showed rats who ate GMO food compared to Non-GMO food were passive at times, irritated at other times, and always anti-social. So companies feed GMO crops to their animals, then we eat those meats ourselves thus consuming those mutated genes, and passing them on. Once Bayer has sold all these GE seeds for GMO products, sprayed those crops with pesticides, herbicides, and fungicides, fed those GMO crops to livestock, and then the farmers sell those GMO crops to various food companies who put them into thousands of processed foods which contribute to cancer, diabetes, etc. etc. etc.... then Bayer sells us their pharmaceuticals to enrich themselves even more.

Bayer sells tons of pharmaceuticals to treat everything from pulmonary hypertension to diabetes. Bayer sells cancer treatment medications like Xofigo and radiation treatments like Medrad. Those medications make Bayer AG huge money. So Bayer AG from start to finish collects money on every aspect. Bayer sells the poisons to us, and then sells us the medications to treat it. That is a beautiful business plan.

Well, I guess if you own stock in Bayer AG it is, but not so much for the rest of us. People are trying to fight back though. Bayer AG/Monsanto is facing some 8,000 lawsuits!

In mid-September, 2018, Bayer AG had to ask a California judge to throw out a 289 million dollar jury verdict due to glyphosate (Roundup) giving cancer to a school groundskeeper, Mr. Dewayne Johnson. The case was fast tracked because Mr. Johnson has Non-Hodgkin's lymphoma and is in extremely poor health. Bayer AG came out with a typical bullshit statement. Bayer stated "The jury's decision is wholly at odds with over 40 years of real-world use, an extensive body of scientific data and analysis... which support the conclusion that glyphosate-based herbicides are safe for use and do not cause cancer in humans." Sure Bayer AG, we believe you. The question is will money win out as usual or will the judge reaffirm the jury's decision. Who knows what kind of deals and discussions will take place behind closed doors. If the judge reaffirms the jury's decision, what kind of effect will that have on all those other lawsuits Bayer AG is facing? It won't be good and I'm worried that a message along with some money will be sent somewhere so that something unjust will happen with Mr. Johnson's verdict. A reasonable compromise was reached considering the jury's large verdict and Mr. Johnson agreed to accept a total of $78 million dollars. That's a lot of money and is awesome, but would you trade your life for $78 million dollars? $500 million dollars? I think unless you wish to die no amount of money could convince you of the trade and with Bayer AG's insane profits there's probably no amount they would have to pay in order to stop poisoning us.

Nestle, the world's largest food company, is another corporation that has figured out how to profit from poisoning us. Nestle is a really interesting company to look at, and it is so clear they figured out how to capitalize from putting poisonous ingredients into their food. Similar to Bayer subsidiaries, Nestle has too many products to list, and of course there is nothing wrong with that in itself. Starting out, what we want to look at with Nestle is some of the ingredients in almost all of their food products that we consume. We can start with some of the ingredients in the popular Hot Pockets.

Hot Pockets are inexpensive, convenient, and don't tell anyone, but years ago I used to really love Hot Pockets. Here is a list of the many ingredients: **Carrageenan**, is an ingredient often used to thicken and stabilize other ingredients in food. The ill effects of carrageenan are somewhat debatable, but there does seem to be some real concerns regarding the thickening agent. Carrageenan may slow blood clotting, and increase bleeding. Carrageenan can cause inflammation and problems with gastrointestinal health. Some researchers have claimed carrageenan is linked to everything from colorectal cancer, liver cancer, to ulcerative colitis. Although some of the information is debatable, and I found an equal amount of studies on both sides of the argument, when it comes to my health I would prefer to err on the side of caution. Fun fact, according to WebMD some people apply carrageenan directly to the skin for discomfort around the anus. Two things regarding that statement. First, visualize that while eating any food containing carrageenan, and you're likely to eat less of it. Second, it states "some people apply carrageenan directly to the skin for discomfort around the anus." The key word being "for," that implies that's why they are applying it.....wtf people. I'm sure that's not the case, but I thought it was funny, anyway.........

Sodium Citrate, used as a food additive for flavor or as a preservative. Sodium citrate issues from this food additive can include muscle twitching, cramps, bloody stools, irritability, vomiting, and weight gain. To be fair the last two side effects can also be attributed to the drunken state you're probably in when reaching for a hot pocket in the first place. **Sodium Nitrate,** another preservative known to increase your risk of heart disease. **Sodium Aluminum Phosphate,** often used as a stabilizer in various processed foods. Aluminum phosphates can be a contributing factor in Alzheimer's disease and other neurodegenerative disorders. **Sodium Phosphate,** another emulsifier. It's strange to me how many of these thickening agents that companies put in our food are also used as medications to relieve constipation.

We've all heard those medication commercials where at the end the announcer runs through the list of horrible side effects that sound so much worse than the actual problem it's trying to treat, you know, like anal bleeding. Anyway, when you're reading this, try to hear that voice at the end of those commercials. (Make sure you read it quick) Possible side effects include: kidney problems, severe stomach/abdominal pain, mood changes, confusion, weakness, swelling of extremities, chest pain, diarrhea, gas, anal bleeding (oh shit), itching of the tongue, face or throat, and finally trouble breathing. See, wasn't that fun? A little? No? Whatever, neither are those symptoms.

Disodium Phosphate, used to regulate the acidity of food, stabilize and maintain the proper moisture level, and wow, another freaking thickening agent. Disodium phosphate also has some non-food uses including as a flame retardant. As usual some of the issues associated with disodium phosphate are upset stomach and diarrhea. At least now it's pretty clear why Hot Pockets make you go to the bathroom. Other concerns from eating processed foods containing disodium phosphate include: kidney disease, heart and lung disease, thyroid issues, liver disease, and finally Addison's disease.

Cysteine Hydrochloride, used as a dough conditioner, increases the dough's elasticity, and helps it rise during baking. I really didn't read anything bad about this as far as your health because it is an amino acid. However, it more than likely comes from human hair bought from barbershops in China. (It's true). Okay, I will end on that light note. There are somewhere near 80 ingredients in a Hot Pocket, and not all are bad but many are.

Many of these ingredients that Nestle adds to our food has links to cancer, type II diabetes, hypertension, obesity, Alzheimer's disease, Parkinson's disease, multiple sclerosis, end stage renal disease, gastrointestinal diseases, and a myriad of other diseases. Okay, now to the point: Nestle is a food company. Nestle is probably like General Mills, or Kellogg and they use many of these ingredients because they are inexpensive. Well, maybe General Mills, Kellogg, Mars, Coca-Cola, Pepsico. all have stock interest in pharmaceutical holdings. Maybe, but unfortunately I couldn't find it. As I stated earlier, this isn't some conspiracy. Bayer and Nestle have direct, clear interest in making us sick, and then treating us, thus making money every step of the way. Perhaps in Nestle's case they saw what was happening, and how the food they produce makes us sick, and instead of changing their poisonous ingredients they jumped aboard the money train. Nestle has subsidiaries, and interests in companies that profit from sick consumers. Nestle Health Science is a wholly owned subsidiary of Nestle which delves into the cure side of the Nestle corporation. Novartis Medical Nutrition is a subsidiary of Nestle who is the second largest supplier in the medical food sector. Vitaflo specializes in nutrition for people with genetic metabolic diseases. Prometheus Laboratories makes devices to diagnose gastrointestinal diseases and cancer. Pamlab offers medical food products for use in nutritional management of patients with mild cognitive impairment, depression, and diabetic peripheral neuropathy. Accera, Inc. discovers and develops innovative clinical applications to address acute and chronic neurodegenerative diseases. Accera, Inc. provides nutrition for individuals with diseases such as Alzheimer's disease. Chi-Med is a Chinese pharmaceutical company that produces products for gastrointestinal health. (Nestle has a 50-50 partnership with Chi-Med) Lastly, Nestle invested 65 million dollars in Seres Therapeutics which develops microbiome therapeutics. Just to give you an idea of what kind of money these companies generate we can look at some of their net sales numbers. In 2017, Novartis reported 49.1 billion dollars in net sales. Prometheus Laboratories generates a little above 400 million in annual revenue. You get the point, Nestle isn't in the pharmaceutical business to lose money, any more than it is in the food business to lose money. The reality is, Nestle shouldn't be in either business to lose money. The problem arises when they are linked to each other, and it's in the pharmaceutical company's best interests for the food portion of the business to help make us sick. That's just sick Nestle.

I wanted to stay focused on the companies I found that are using poisonous ingredients and causing us to become sick, but I feel remiss if I didn't at least mention the dangers of sugar. Sugar is in 80% of the grocery products we buy. Companies figured out how much sugar to put into their products so we crave them, and sugar also makes the product itself taste pretty awesome.

However, sugar is horrible for you. For years fat has been made out to be the bigger enemy, but if you're consuming healthy fats it's not true. Sugar is in everything so when you're reading those labels be on a sugar count look out. Sugar is linked to an increased risk in diseases such as heart disease, type 2 diabetes, cancer and obesity. Sugar has both physical and psychological effects on us. Anyway, you get it. Do yourself a favor and limit the amount of sugar you intake as much as you possibly can. I promise you, you will be so much healthier for having done so.

Conclusion

As usual, money is in the driver's seat here so anyone that is supposed to be looking out for us isn't. The FDA allows carcinogens like sodium nitrite and sodium nitrate to be added to processed meats, and other foods to preserve them. Caramel color in soda is a known carcinogen, but go ahead and add that too. Microwave popcorn are in bags lined with chemicals, and the seeds themselves have harmful chemicals on them as well. Hydrogenated oils cause cancer, and hydrogenated oils are in tons of products. I used to go through container after container of Nestle's Coffee-mate. I loved Coffee-mate and when I was younger I just assumed a nice wholesome sounding company with a corporate image like Nestle would never put garbage like that in their products. One of my favorite sayings is 'youth is wasted on the young,' and isn't that the truth, especially when it comes to what we put in our bodies. (Including drugs) Coffee-mate has Corn syrup solids, hydrogenated vegetable oil, sodium caseinate, dipotassium phosphate, mono diglycerides, sodium aluminosilicate and God knows what else. I still haven't been able to find a great tasting, decently healthy coffee creamer. Damn it, Nestle!

It's not just Bayer AG and Nestle who are evil; it's all these corporations who find ways to profit from our misery. JP Morgan Chase has huge stakes in the healthcare industries. General Mills owns more than 100 food brands. General Mills CEO from 2007 to 2017 was Kendall Powell, and Mr. Powell also serves on a number of boards including Medtronic and Catalyst. Medtronic is a heart disease and diabetes medical company which makes the number 1 selling insulin pump. Wouldn't it be in Mr. Powell's best interest to make sure most of those General Mills food brands contributed to individuals obesity, increasing heart disease, and diabetes? Catalyst is even worse. Actually, I'm joking, well, unless you're of the mindset of a Donald Trump. That's because Catalyst is actually a pretty awesome organization which works to help put women into leadership roles at various companies across the globe. So maybe Mr. Powell isn't exactly a bad person, but never underestimate the power of money, and an individual's greed. Mr. Powell is obviously an intelligent, informed individual who surely understands what harmful ingredients are going into General Mills products, and what diseases those ingredients cause. General Mills' Fiber One Bars is the comparative example I always use when speaking to someone about what these companies are doing to their consumers. Fiber One Bars are products that if you are purchasing them, you are assuming you are buying a very healthy product, but Fiber One Bars contain approximately 30 ingredients, including too much sugar. In comparing all the ingredients in a Fiber One Bar to a Lara Bar, there is no comparison. Lara Bars usually have 2 to 4 ingredients, and you can actually read the ingredients, and know what they are by name. (No need to Google).

As I stated earlier, the FDA isn't looking out for us as they both have a revolving door, and are bought and paid for. Let's look at some other trusted organizations that are supposed to want what's best for us. The American Diabetes Association, nope. The American Cancer Society, nope. The American Heart Association, nope. How about the trusted Susan G. Komen Foundation? Nope, nope, nope, and nope. Clearly, I'm not saying these organizations just do horrible things, but they do follow the money. All four organizations are funded in part by the food industry, and the pharmaceutical industry. All four organizations also promote diets filled with beef and dairy, both of which are contributors to the very diseases these organizations are fighting. Our government isn't looking out for our best interest either. As discussed previously, our legislators get large campaign contributions from Big Pharma, and the food industry so they aren't going to stop these companies from putting known carcinogens in our food.

For fucks sake, our local governments are still putting fluoride into are water supply. Fluoride shouldn't be ingested. Fluoride should be applied topically by a dentist. The fluoride that is added to our water isn't the same as the fluoride found in some water, nor is it a pharmaceutical grade fluoride which your dentist would use. Instead, the fluoride is an unprocessed industrial byproduct of the phosphate fertilizer industry. This type of fluoride often contains elevated levels of arsenic. Have you ever looked at the back of your toothpaste box? Look at it, go ahead, I'll wait................ Forget it, I'll just tell you. "Warning: Keep out of the reach of children under 6 yrs of age. If more than used for brushing is accidentally swallowed, get medical help or contact the Poison Control Center right away." Ingesting a tablespoon of fluoride could potentially kill a child. Make no mistake about it, fluoride is a poison. Why is our government putting it into our water supply? Simple, the fluoride industry, like every other industry has lobbyists, and those lobbyists contribute money to those in power who keep the bs narrative alive. We've all heard the saying "tell a lie long enough, and it becomes the truth," and that is exactly what is happening here. Confront someone with the truth about fluoride, and they most likely won't believe you. The reason being that it's hard to truly change your mindset about something you've always believed in, and have always been told. It's the same reason someone like myself has trouble going from agnostic to full blown atheist.

It's up to us to stop this poisoning. I'm a vegetarian for personal, moral reasons, and people will often say "yeah, but one person isn't going to make a difference." Yes, that's true, if I were the only fucking person! It's simple supply and demand. The more vegetarians there are, the more demand there will be for vegetarian products, and the less demand there will be for meat. It's the exact same way with organic products. I try to buy everything I can that's organic. Not that many years ago, the organic section in a supermarket was small to non-existent. Now when I go to the supermarket the organic section is pretty significant. Organic products aren't that much more expensive. Buy organic, cut down on your meat consumption. If you eat meat four days a week, reduce the number to two or three days a week. In the last ten years, meat consumption has risen by almost 20%. One-fifth of all the greenhouse gas emissions which are man-made come from the meat industry. If you can believe it, that means all those cows, and pigs, etc. are passing so much gas that they produce more greenhouse emissions than the transportation sector. I actually have a friend I believe is contributing quite a bit to these greenhouse emissions as well, but

I'm pretty sure his diet is the main reason for that.

Each pound of meat produced also takes huge amounts of water. Each pound of meat produced takes about 10 times the amount of water as some vegetables. If everyone in the United States were vegan for one day a week, it would be as if we magically reduced our collective driving miles by nearly 100 billion miles. The point is; yes, you, as an individual can make a difference because we don't live in a bubble. It's you, and you, and you, and together we are more powerful than even a lobbyist!

Do yourself a favor and be a label reader and use my favorite app called Yuka, which has made the biggest change to my eating habits ever. The app is life changing! It tells you what hazardous chemicals are in the food you want to buy and what that chemical does to you. So now when I go to buy something, I scan it and when I see it has X amount of cancer causing ingredients in it I don't buy it. It's honestly difficult to buy something once you see the horrible ingredients. Peanut M&Ms were one of my favorite candies to eat, but not anymore. Call the 800 numbers on the backs of the product boxes and tell them you want them to stop using a poisonous ingredient when you see it. Stop buying their products! Does it help overnight? No, it takes time. I love Triscuits, but I stopped buying them because they use canola oil, however organic Triscuits do not. I make my voice heard by buying organic Triscuits, and if that's something you care about then you should make your voice heard too. It takes time but in the end the numbers won't lie to these companies. You buy "this", and don't buy "that" then eventually those corporations will produce much, much more of "this" and much less of "that."

You Say You Want a Revolution……well

A billionaire, a middle class worker, and an immigrant are sitting at a table with 1000 cookies. The billionaire takes 999 cookies and turns to the middle class worker and says, "you better watch it, that immigrant is going to take your cookie."

I'm not sure who came up with that, but I love it, and you can change "immigrant" to a single mother getting food stamps or anyone else getting any type of help. That saying sums up exactly what billionaires/Republicans, try to frame the way of thinking to an easily manipulated, large portion of middle class Americans. The greed of guys like Amazon's Jeff Bezos has got to stop. This guy should be strung up by his balls, swinging from a tree. Most of us live paycheck to paycheck, and I know for myself I can't get out of the crushing burden of my student loans. Okay, we may not want the kind of revolution where we string up guys like Bezos, or do we?? Fine, how about we get Congress to pass Bernie Sanders and Ro Khanna's bill to tax corporations like Amazon, and Walmart for every dollar their low-wage workers receive in government assistance. It will be interesting to see if the rest of the Democrats get behind this obviously fair, and needed bill or will they let the corporations control them as usual.

We need Bernie to be the Donald Trump of the Democratic Party, and bend the party to his will. It started happening, and we were getting stronger, and stronger with more, and more left leaning candidates winning Democratic primaries, and elections. However, the movement seems to have lost its steam. People have been so distracted with Covid and everything is so politicized that too many people are content with picking one of the two sides. I'm sure the Democrats and the Republicans are very happy about this. Most people who are left of the Democrats and who have the guts to criticize the Democrats get ostracized. Take someone like Jimmy Dore or Russel Brand. I love listening to them both and they are the furthest thing from Republicans but yet people aligned with the Democrats can't stand them. I'd be happy to be associated with either of those two free thinking gentlemen. We have to get the party moving to the left or we need to have these candidates running as Independents. If the Democratic Party doesn't come aboard, who cares? If "The Squad" is truly who they portrayed themselves to be then they need to stop playing nice and branch out and expand. We need a legitimate third party to be the norm. Having a real third party is the only way we can possibly get corruption out of politics. So, news outlets I challenge you to start giving coverage to third party candidates. Come on Chris Cuomo, Wolf Blitzer, Alisyn Camerota, and John Berman. Come on Brian Williams, Ali Velshi, and Andrea Mitchell. Come on my hero Bill Maher. Come on Tucker Carlson, and Sean Hannity, okay, there's only a 5% chance the people I listed will ever cover third party candidates, and that drops to zero for Fox Fake News.

One thing I do want to make crystal clear; I don't dislike our troops. I respect them, and what they believe in. It's those in power who lie to them that I dislike. I believe in truly supporting our troops, not just giving lip service to it. Politicians love doing that but then they often desert them upon their return from war. Our troops were deserted after the Vietnam War. Our troops were deserted after Operation Desert Storm where our government denied the existence of Gulf War Syndrome.

Of the almost 700,000 troops who served in the Gulf War, approximately 250,000 troops suffered from Gulf War Syndrome. I believe the best way our government can support our troops is to not put them in harm's way for no reason. That's what I want for our troops. If a U.S. soldier is going to risk their life, then it needs to be something worth risking it for, not for oil or our corporation's profits. It needs to be a just war, i.e. WWII. I don't criticize this country because I hate it, I criticize the United States government because I love our country. I just want it to be as beautiful as its ideals are. I want those in power to represent the people, not the corporations. I don't really want to string Jeff Bezos up by his balls. First off, sorry Jeff, but I'm not touching your balls. Mr. Bezos just announced he's going to raise his starting pay to $15.00 an hour, which is a great start. Mr. Bezos is still way too greedy though. I started writing this book being motivated by anger. I want to see change. I can't take all these injustices any more. Maybe it won't help at all. Maybe I can make a small difference in writing this book. We can all make small changes and together make a difference.

Writing this book has been emotionally painful at times, but it has also been therapeutic. During the Trump administration, our country is more polarized than ever. I've lost many friends who I've known for years. They weren't the person I thought they were and I have been vocal in my calling out of Trump and any racist or immoral behavior. I guess I've insulted many, and in return their ignorance and racism broke my heart. There were times while researching I had to stop, and take a deep breath. The people who suffer at the hands of our might are real people. I saw many disturbing photos. Sometimes the photos were of Noam Chomsky's "unpeople" who were missing limbs from bombs dropped years ago. Sometimes the heartbreaking photos were of children crying over their dead mother or father's body. We go about our lives, and what do we worry about? Getting a better job or maybe a nicer car? Our problems are real, but unless a family member is sick with cancer or something along those lines, our problems tend to revolve around material things we don't have. What most Americans pray for is so different compared to what someone who was born in a third world country worries about.

If there has been an "unpeople" here in the United States, I suppose that would be African Americans. There is no shortage of heartbreaking photos or films revolving around the treatment of African Americans. From lynchings to beatings just because the color of their skin. I love the movies Mississippi Burning, A Time to Kill, Birth of a Nation, 12 Years A Slave, and The Help. Watching those movies is emotionally draining, but they aren't fiction, and they aren't ancient history either. One of my top five favorite books ever is Frederick Douglass's My Bondage and My Freedom. My Bondage and My Freedom should be mandatory reading for every high school student. I think it could go a long way to eliminating any racist thoughts. It is such a powerful book, and can be life altering. Education and knowledge are always the key. Knowledge of what's happening throughout the world. Knowledge about what's happening in our own country. If you see the hypocrisy, if you see the truth, how can you not want to make a change?

Public Service Announcements

Stop laughing at the phrase "Do your own research"

Doing your own research means you are reading what experts are saying then you are deciding who you agree with. No one who says they did their own research or tells someone else to do their own research is doing experiments, they are just reading, asshole!

Don't Impede My Right to Speed, if you are in the fast lane, speed or as Ludacris said "move bitch, get out the way, get out the way bitch, get out the way." Seriously, if the speed limit is 65 and you're in the fast lane doing 60 or 65 you should be shot. Yes, really, shot! (Okay, shot at?? Just to really scare them, then a good talking to?)

Say "thank you" when a stranger holds open the door for you, rudeness infuriates me! Do you think it's someone's job to open the door for you? No, it isn't so if a stranger holds the door for you, says thank you, or you are obviously a complete, rude, asshole.

Use Face Lotion, if you don't use lotion on your face you probably look ten years older than you are, or than you should. Do yourself, and everyone else a favor, and use lotion.

Put Your Article All On One Page, If I google an article, and then I go to read it, and have to keep hitting "Next," and "Next," and "Next," then guess what? I'm not reading that shit!

Get a Real Job State Troopers, stop stealing the money of hard working people just trying to get to work on time. You steal our money so you can have a paycheck. You're the biggest welfare collector of all.

When Going Up An Onramp to Get on the Throughway……..Look!!!!!!,
Don't wait til you're at the last 50 feet of the onramp and then start panicking, looking how you're going to get in the lane. Look as you're going up the onramp, you not-knowing-how-to-drive mother fuckers!

Stop Texting While Driving!, I have to drive a lot for my job and I can't believe how many people I see with their heads down, staring at their phone, texting away and never, ever looking up. You're going to kill someone! I always hope they have a close call that will wake them up and make them see the text can seriously wait.

Student Loans!, 20 years after I graduated, and I still owe over $60,000 dollars in student loans. For 6 straight years I had been paying over $300.00 a month with not one penny going toward the principle. Other years I've paid less and sometimes nothing depending on my financial situation. Student loans are financial slavery for over 44 million Americans who owe approximately 1.5 trillion dollars! Instead of bailing out the banks our government should bail out those with student loans. It would allow those millions of Americans to spend more money in their communities, improving the lives of themselves and many others in the process. (Sorry, that one wasn't really a PSA, but I hate the feeling of drowning in my never ending student loan debt and I had to vent).

About the Author

James considers himself a Bill Maher type of Liberal, (well, maybe not any more).I listen to Russel Brand and Jimmy Dore a lot more these days. In other words, he's going to speak the truth, and if you're offended you might need to toughen up or go get a hug or something. Oftentimes liberals' unwillingness to speak the truth for fear of looking as if they are not the super liberal they think they are just stops things from getting done and the truth from being told. James earned a Bachelor's degree in History from the University at Buffalo, and a Master's degree in Secondary Education from Niagara University. James was a professional boxer, and although talented for various reasons James ended up a journeyman fighter. James, along with Ken Cosentino, Liz Cosentino, and Baird Hageman own the film production company "White Lion Studios." James starred in "Crimson: The Motion Picture", and had a supporting role in the hilarious "Attack of the Killer

Shrews!" James also owns the t-shirt company Tortured Tees. Tortured Tees are designed for motorcycle and tattoo enthusiasts. Tortured Tees, for the tortured soul in all of us. James hopes this book is both entertaining and educational, and inspires you to make any small change which will create a small, but significant difference in someone's life.

Made in the USA
Middletown, DE
17 September 2023

38668960R00126